I0762930

PRAISE FOR *NORTH OF ORDINARY*

"*North of Ordinary* is a page-turner of a memoir, a stunning portrait of Alaska, and an adventure story unlike any other. Sue Aikens's grit and determination shine through, lighting the way for anyone chasing resilience against the odds."

—Mariana van Zeller, investigative journalist for National Geographic

"If you've ever wondered how it would feel to take on a life in remote Alaska with the 'real world' far away, read *North of Ordinary*. This ain't some polished-up, made-for-TV wilderness tale; it's the raw, bloody, bone-deep truth. Sue Aikens lays it all bare—grit, grief, guts, and grace—in a voice so honest it'll chill you like an Arctic wind. This book isn't just authentic...it *is* Alaska."

—Roland Welker, winner of season 7 of *Alone*

"I've spent over a decade telling stories on camera with Sue in her home of remote Alaska. Over the course of these adventures, I was often convinced I knew where they were headed. And more often than not, those expectations were diverted by surprising and uncanny events—usually for the better. I had the same experience reading *North of Ordinary*. Sue is a one-in-a-million kind of person, and I consider myself lucky to have shared part of my life with her. I hope you feel the same way as you read this book and she shares her life with you."

—Daniel Espy, *Life Below Zero* producer

"If Sue's life were the standard for which an autobiography could be written, not much else could ever be justifiably penned, I'm afraid. A term she uses only once in this book made me chuckle—'Alaskan easy.' It's likely you already know her life is anything but easy. However, once you complete this dive into the testimony of her days, you will think of her in two ways—as a sister in brokenness and joy to whom you can relate, and as a winter warrior who will leave you in a state of awe."

—John Paul Bensley, author of *Finnegan*

"Sue Aikens doesn't just survive—she thrives. *North of Ordinary* is a fierce, deeply human reminder that life is lived one step at a time and that the wildest journeys begin with the courage to seek more."

—Luke Neumayr, owner of V8 Ranch

"I met Sue Aikens thirteen years ago, and what began as a working relationship quickly grew into a bond that went far beyond coworkers—we became family. Over the years, I watched her journey from living alone nine months out of the year in the remote Alaskan wilderness to becoming a television icon, with our show earning twenty Emmy nominations and nine wins along the way. Through it all, Sue never changed. People often ask me, 'What's Sue really like?' and unlike most reality television personalities, I can honestly say she is exactly the same person you see on-screen: tough, funny, fiercely independent, and deeply true to herself. This book is Sue—unfiltered, unflinching, and unforgettable."

—Joseph Litzinger, Emmy-nominated TV producer

"*North of Ordinary* is a memoir of grit, wilderness, and the unforgiving north. Sue Aikens's fascinating journey is part survival manual, part personal testimony, and all heart. It's about making choices when there's no safety net, no lifeline, and no way out but through. It's about resilience that isn't pretty but somehow works. If you want the truth about what it costs—and what it gives back—to live a life where comfort is never guaranteed, this is it. Raw. Relentless. Real.

"Sue doesn't just tell survival stories; she lives them. From the Alaskan tundra to the courtroom of public opinion, she's built a reputation on grit, scars, and her uncanny ability to say what others won't. *North of Ordinary* is her no-spin testimony of what it takes to live beyond the safety net. I have met Sue in the high Arctic tundra, and I interviewed her there in Kavik. But after reading this book, I feel like I know the depth of her too."

—Greta Van Susteren, journalist and news anchor

"Sue's story is a blueprint of how hard work, determination, and sticking to your values will overcome the very toughest of challenges in life. She makes you believe that you are right there with her as she navigates her extraordinary story. Reading this book has made me want to take on life's biggest challenges right now! It's a book for all age groups and should be in every school in the nation."

—Cara Darmody, Irish disability rights campaigner

"Reading *North of Ordinary* offers a rare perspective into the extraordinary and unusual life Sue has lived: an unforgettable journey that resonates beyond Alaska. I have known Sue for over a decade and have witnessed the 'Beauty and the Beast' element of the Alaskan wilderness. Reading the details and picturing the moments will put any reader straight into the many stimulating adventures she has gone through. *North of Ordinary* reveals the essence of her personality and the tenacity of her soul in an unforgettable life's journey."

—Michael Cheeseman, *Life Below Zero* cinematographer

NORTH OF ORDINARY

NORTH OF ORDINARY

HOW ONE WOMAN LEFT IT ALL BEHIND FOR WILDERNESS AND WONDER IN ALASKA'S FROZEN FRONTIER

SUE AIKENS

WITH MICHAEL VLESSIDES

Cover design by James Iacobelli
Author photograph by Jayce Kolinski © 2024 BBC STUDIOS
Background image © Dan Ballard/Getty Images
Internal design by Tara Jaggers/Sourcebooks

Published by Sourcebooks
1935 Brookdale RD, Naperville, IL 60563-2773
(630) 961-3900
sourcebooks.com

Cataloging-in-Publication Data is on file with the Library of Congress.

Printed and bound in the United States of America.
VP 10 9 8 7 6 5 4 3 2 1

CHAPTER 1

ALONE

I was alone.

Alone. It was the singular, heart-achingly obvious, and now-irrefutable characteristic that defined the whole of my existence. I was only twelve years old, but my life had been reduced to a single point of reference. There was no past and no future, only the there and then. And in the there and then, in the middle of the Alaskan wilderness, a place my mother had moved me just a scant couple of weeks before, there was nobody but me.

I'd been alone a lot to that point in my life, but now my isolation was on display in a way that I'd never before experienced. In my former life, one that now seemed light-years away, I'd often been on my own, but I was better able to mask the grim reality of my place in the world behind the daily machinations of life with my five siblings, my mother, and the men she called her husbands. But here in the deep and mythical forests of Alaska, my aloneness took on an entirely different significance.

Back in Illinois, in the Chicago suburbs that our family traversed with a regularity that could only be called nomadic, I was merely a kid on the outside. But the trappings of my childhood in the 1960s and '70s, as short and tumultuous and unpredictable as it was, still meant that I was able to entertain myself in other ways, ways that did not usually demand the love or approval of the people closest to me. I always had something to do, someplace new to explore, and even other people to occasionally fill the void in my heart. But here no such backdrop existed. Here it was all on display for everybody and nobody to see. There was no hiding from it, no escaping the fact that little Susie Moore had become just another creature on the great Alaskan food chain struggling to survive. Suddenly I was profoundly insignificant in the ancient workings of the deep, relentless, savage, and all-knowing wilderness around me, a thing so much bigger than me that I felt like it would swallow me up right then and there, eradicating any memory of the fact that I had ever existed at all.

I was alone.

That realization washed over me like a tidal wave. It started somewhere far away but slowly built momentum as it made its way across the world until it reached that exact spot where I lay on the ground, a tear-stained kid who only wanted for her mother—her *mother*, for god's sake—to come scoop her up and tell her everything was going to be OK. But she didn't. She wouldn't. I knew she wouldn't because she never had. I was alone. *Alonealonealonealonealonealone.*

And while I couldn't see it at the time through the tears and the dirt and the snot smeared across my face, my mother had somehow charted a course for me that would ultimately define the rest of my life. In some way, I would always be alone. Yet at the same time, through some magical twist of biology that is the inner workings of my brain, I would never, *ever* feel lonely.

I scraped myself off the forest floor that had been my bed for the past two nights and brushed the dirt and leaves and pine needles off my clothes as best I could.

"All right," I said. "Let's do this."

Less than a month before, I had little, if any, notion of what Alaska was beyond the general knowledge that most fifth graders have of the untamed and mysterious land that serves as the spiritual capstone of the United States. My life was in Illinois, and as screwed up and disjointed as it may have been, it was unabashedly *mine*, and as I grew up, I learned to revel in my ownership of my existence. From a very young age, I recognized that there was something special in being able to look past the difficulties that festooned daily life and find joy in the things that others considered mundane.

The old oak tree at the edge of my street, its trunk split open by lightning long before I was born, became a hidden fortress, a space where I could simply sit and listen to the wind rush through the leaves. The creek that ran behind the rows of houses, largely ignored by the other kids in the neighborhood, was more like a kingdom to me than a narrow trickle of water choked with weeds and lined with old stones. Even the abandoned field at the edge of town became a place where I could lie down in peace and watch the clouds pass overhead. These were the places where I didn't need to explain myself, where my existence was celebrated, not just tolerated. The wind and the water and the grass didn't care who I was. They accepted me as *me*, and that was enough.

Such distractions aside, my childhood was far from easy. By the time I was a toddler in the mid-1960s, my family had moved often enough to dispel any notion that my upbringing was going to be one of stability and normalcy. We started out in Mundelein, Illinois, headed west to Las Vegas for a bit, and then landed back in the Chicago area.

There were eight of us back then, before things got screwy and my family scattered to the four winds: Mom and Jack, along with my five much-older siblings Charlie, Vicki, Steve, and the twins, Sandy and Pam. I was the youngest but never enjoyed the distinction of being babied. Instead, I was the family outcast, a wolf culled from the herd at birth. There were family trips that I didn't go on, family meals I didn't partake in, family holidays where I was present but ignored.

This may have had something to do with the fact that the identity of my biological father was a mystery to everyone but my mother. To this day she's never told me who he was, a fact she insists is completely immaterial in my day-to-day life. I've accepted the fact that I'll likely never know him and have come to terms with that mystery. My life is in the here and now, not the smoke and haze of the past. As I like to say, if you've got one foot in yesterday and the other in tomorrow, you're only pissing on today.

But it sure would've been nice to know him when I was a child because at least then I would have felt a positive emotional connection to a male role model. Instead, all I had in those early years was Jack Moore, the tough-as-nails, no-nonsense Chicago cop whose name somehow made it onto my birth certificate from Holy Family Hospital in Des Plaines, Illinois.

Even so, I never called him *Dad*, like the other kids did. To me, he was always just Jack, which is exactly how he wanted it. Jack didn't need to tell me that I wasn't a part of him because his actions did that on their own. I was a ghost to him, the shadow that lived in the house but one he rarely acknowledged. Not that Charlie, Vicki, Steve, Sandy, and Pam had some kind of idyllic upbringing like the Brady Bunch kids I watched on TV. Jack was an imposing presence, and there were a lot of fights. A lot of screaming. A lot of drinking. And a lot of hitting. But at the very least, my siblings went to sleep at night knowing who their father was and that he was there under the same roof as them.

I wasn't sad when Jack was erased from my life. Mom told me he died, but I soon realized from the way my siblings talked that it was a lie. *Buggered off,* I overhead them say among themselves. I never found out if he and Mom got divorced because I never knew if they were married in the first place. Mom wasn't one for tradition, especially ones that put women "in their place," as men of that generation liked to say. When it came to men, she was a free spirit. *Make love, not war, man.* Jack quickly became a memory, and Mom said nothing more about him. It was almost like he never existed, except for the fact that his children filled our household.

My mother could be alluring when she wanted to be, and attracting men came easily to her. The months after Jack left saw a steady stream of them visit our house, rough-and-tumble guys who never stayed for very long and seemed even less interested in my existence than Jack had been. But one of them, a man named Joe, stayed. In fact, Joe stayed so long that he actually married my mother, an act that forever changed my view of him as a person and of them as a couple. I was seven years old, and in my childhood innocence, I believed that marriage was forever, so I let Joe into my heart.

The best part about Joe was that he liked me too. In fact, he liked me so much that he actually allowed me to call him *Dad*. To Joe, I was on equal footing with the rest of the kids. He hadn't fathered *any* of us, so there was no biological reason for him to distinguish me from anyone else.

Joe was a roofer in the Chicago area. His buddies and coworkers called him The Squirrel because of his fearless ability to scamper around the top of Chicago's tallest buildings without a second thought. Not everyone in the family held such a high opinion of Joe as I did, though. My brothers and sisters said he worked for the Chicago mob, but that didn't matter one bit to me. Joe was the closest thing I ever had to a dad, and I wasn't going to let something as peripheral as the Mafia get in the way of that. When Joe came home from work, he actually looked for me and smiled when he saw me. When I think of Joe, I think of chicken soup, which is what he smelled like...super salty, but someone you'd like to share crackers with.

Like Jack before him, Joe was an incredibly strong man, which sometimes made him scary. He liked to say he was "old school," which meant that you paid the price if you disrespected him or my mother. For me, that meant occasionally getting picked up by the ankles and hung upside down in one of Joe's meaty hands while he took the belt to my sorry ass. If I was lucky, I only got the leather. Sometimes I got the buckle, though, and that's when things got really unpleasant. That said, I never took the beatings personally.

All the other kids I knew got hit by their parents when they did something wrong; that's just the way things were back then. So hitting or not, I cared about Joe.

I could handle the physical punishment. In some ways, Joe's beatings were predictable, with a defined cause and effect that fit with my vision of the way the world worked. *For every action there was an equal and opposite reaction.* It was physics, and I could understand that. Plus, I wasn't singled out. Joe beat all us kids with equal regularity.

What confounded me much more than the occasional belt to my bottom was my mother. Like any child, I wanted to be loved, fully and unconditionally, by her. I was trying to make sense of the world around me as I was growing up and desperately wanted someone to help me through it all. I wanted to hold her hand as we walked down the street and she pointed things out to me, like the other moms did. I wanted her to escort me to the bus stop, kiss me on the cheek, and wave to me as I pressed my face against the window and watched her fade into the distance. I wanted her to read me a bedtime story, pull the covers up to my chin, and then flick the light off as she closed the door softly behind her. As I got older, I wanted her to teach me about geography and math and puberty and cooking and tampons and boys and hygiene and love. But she was too busy struggling with her own demons to give me what I needed.

She was—and is—an enigma. Beautiful and mysterious, my mother could go toe-to-toe in an intellectual battle of wits with anyone. She also had her softer moments, rare occasions where she showed me genuine kindness, vulnerability, and love. In those instances, I felt as though I was the only person in the world. But she was unable to maintain that sort of emotional connection for any length of time, and I invariably watched her backslide into a shadow of that same person. As a result, I felt like I was constantly tiptoeing through the minefield of my mother's emotions. Would she embrace me or tell me I was the devil's child? More often than not, it was the latter.

There was no bedtime story on those occasions, no gentle closing of the door as I drifted off to sleep dreaming of the characters that had been conjured in my head. Instead, my mother put me to bed by explaining to me in vivid detail what a terrible person I was.

"Who could love you?" she'd say. "Just look at you. You're stupid and lazy. Oh sure, cry. Go ahead… Maybe then you'll wear yourself out and go to sleep. If you really loved anyone but yourself, you would just stop. *Stop!*"

But I couldn't stop, and I think she probably knew that from experience. The sobs came in heaving waves, a torrent of emotion I released from somewhere deep inside that would not relent until they hit the cool air outside my body. If I cried hard enough, I would experience some kind of neurological short circuit and pass out. Years later, that reaction would be diagnosed as something called a psychogenic nonepileptic seizure, a seizure-like attack that's the product of underlying psychological distress instead of abnormal electrical activity in the brain. For me, the underlying psychological distress was my mother.

So that's how I went to sleep, almost every fucking night.

Yet even in those moments, with my mother towering over me and telling me some of the most destructive things imaginable, I never hated her. I hated what she was doing; I hated the power her words had over me. But at the same time, I knew that no matter how badly she treated me—and there were some doozies—she was always just doing the best she could. She had six children to raise, not a lot of money to do it, and little help from the outside world.

Is this the way I would have scripted my childhood? No. But that doesn't necessarily make it bad. In the end, those experiences made me who I am. And looking back, I'm OK with the way it turned out because it made me the person I am today. I'm flawed, to be sure. I have scars and bumps and bruises that live inside me every day. Psychologists say I have the emotional development of a seven- or eight-year-old, and I guess that checks out. But I have crafted my life so the skeletons of my past are locked in a closet, which allows me to focus on the beauty around me. We all carry emotional baggage. I just choose to put that Gucci shit down and move on.

As I began to grow up and the 1970s arrived, I increasingly found solace in school. For seven or eight hours each day, I was able to experience the world on my own terms, not those of my family. Slowly I began to develop a sense of who I was and where I fit in the world. I knew what it felt like to be mistreated and didn't want to see other people, especially kids, go through the same thing. I began to view myself as a bit of a superhero, a loner child who defended the weak, the unappreciated, and the overlooked. I was one among them, so I knew well their plight.

My exposure to the greater world around me also introduced me to people outside the circle of my family. No longer was my universe limited to Mom, Joe, Steve, Sandy, and Pam. (Charlie, much older than me, moved out when I was still a toddler, and Vicki had gone off to college.) The best part about that introduction was that I realized that there were people out there who actually thought I had something to offer. For perhaps the first time in my life, I began to think of myself as more than just an outcast.

Of those people, none was more important than Mrs. McCaskey, the soft-spoken woman who tutored me at home for several months in third grade after I came down with a nasty combination of illnesses like rheumatic fever and the Hong Kong flu. I could feel Mrs. McCaskey's warmth the moment she walked into our house for the first time; it was an invisible force she radiated that touched everyone in the room, though I felt like it was meant just for me. The thing I loved most about Mrs. McCaskey was that she was genuinely interested in what I had to say; she treated me like an intelligent person whose opinions and views of the world were valid.

We worked through our lessons at a rapid pace each day and then spent the rest of our time together simply talking and enjoying one another's company. When I told her I wanted to be a marine biologist, she came back the next day with books about the oceans. When I said I wanted to learn how to cook, she showed up with *The Betty Crocker Cookbook.* Mrs. McCaskey said I saw the world differently than most people, but she didn't think that was a problem.

"Sue," she said, putting an arm around me one afternoon and holding me close enough that I could smell her perfume, "don't ever let anybody tell you that you're not smart. Don't ever let anybody tell you that you can't dream and that what you want isn't good enough. If you start believing that you can't, you won't. You *are* smart, and you *are* allowed to dream."

As awful as it was to be sick, I was sad to get well again because I knew it meant my time with Mrs. McCaskey would finish, which it eventually did. I hated to say goodbye to the first adult who made me feel valued as an individual, but in the end, Mrs. McCaskey gave me so much more than knowledge; she gave me hope that the reality of my childhood was a small part in the much larger mosaic of my life. So when she came and went like a wind through the trees, I held on to the lessons she taught me for dear life.

The memories of our time together were precious to me, and I used them to bolster my spirit every time I needed to be lifted beyond the challenges of home life, which came with alarming regularity. If you did something wrong in our house, you got your ass beat. This was a universal fact. The sun rises, and then it sets. You screw up, you get beat. Simple.

I wasn't alone in this, though. Middle-American discipline in the 1970s seemed to be as much a physical act as anything else, and the other kids in school talked about it too. But I must have gotten more beatings than your average kid because one evening a couple of official-looking people with briefcases rang the doorbell and asked to see my parents.

Mom and Joe took them into the living room, where they all sat down and talked. I hid around the corner in the hallway, leaning my head close enough to the doorway to hear what they were saying but just far enough away that nobody knew I was there. Somehow, the visitors had caught wind of the fact that I had more bruises than other kids and wanted to make sure everything was OK in our household. Mom and Joe told them I was just a klutzy kid who fell a lot.

After about a half hour of such talk, the man and woman thanked Mom and Joe for their time, got up, and left. Nothing much changed after that, though. The sun rose, and it set. And if you screwed up, you got your ass beat. The universe was still aligned. The people with the briefcases came back to our house a few more times over the next year or two. Each time, I hid in the hallway and listened their conversation, and each time they left as quietly as they had come. And nothing much at home changed.

I wanted it to, though. I wanted it to change so badly I could taste it. I wanted my mother to look at me like Mrs. McCaskey did, like I was more than just a tumor. I wanted Joe to stop hitting me every time I messed up. I wanted Steve and Sandy and Pam to love me and include me and protect me. But they didn't, and it stung. At the same time, though, I was fiercely loyal to each of them. There were a lot of dysfunction and cruelty in our household, but at least it was *our* dysfunction and cruelty. On those nights when the man and woman visited our house, I stood in the hallway, a nine-year-old conflicted. I wanted to cry *Save me!* at one moment and *Get the hell out of our house!* the next.

I worked hard to be loved. I told myself that if I was a good kid and did well in school, people would love me more. But they didn't. In the fifth grade, I brought home my report card, buzzing with excitement at my success: seven A's and one B. It wasn't perfect, but all things considered, I was ecstatic. Until I got home and showed it to Mom, that is. I proudly handed her the piece of paper, only to watch her face twist into a scowl as she read through it.

"You got a B in science?" she said. "You're not trying hard enough. When are you ever gonna amount to anything? With grades like this, you think you're gonna amount to something? You're not even fucking trying."

I can't say my mother's reaction came as a surprise; I had gotten used to the fact that most things I did fell short of her expectations. At the same time, though, I was crushed. I had convinced myself that by succeeding at school, I would finally show my mother I was a good person. A smart person. A valuable person. As her words spilled out of her mouth, I felt my heart tighten in my chest. I wanted to run away, find Mrs. McCaskey, and have her pull me close enough that I could smell her perfume again. I wanted somebody—*anybody*—to tell me I was good. I retreated to my room and buried my face in my pillow, sobbing. I had so wanted to win my mom's approval and had actually convinced myself that this might be the time.

I took my face out of my pillow, sat up on my bed, and took a deep breath. I was eleven years old, old enough to recognize that my family life was not going to change. No matter how hard I tried, nothing made a difference. I was an outsider looking in and likely always would be. I stood up, looked in the mirror, and spoke to myself.

"Sue, you're *not* the problem," I said quietly yet firmly. "*They're* the problem."

In that moment—on the day I brought home a report card with seven A's and one B—I committed to a reality that I have held on to every day of my life ever since: There is no champion for me other than myself. I resolved to not let anybody bring me down, no matter how much they tried. I had been nurturing thoughts of independence and self-love for as long as I could remember, but from that day forward, I would somehow make them a reality.

In some ways, the realization that I could only count on myself buoyed me. By letting go of the notion that others would care for me and love me, I stopped looking for it. Of course, I still had to navigate the tumultuous waters of my household, but there were fewer personalities to work around as I was the only child left by that time. Charlie had long since moved to Alaska; Vicki was still in college. As for Steve, Sandy, and Pam, they had all gotten married and moved away despite the fact that they were all still teenagers.

The departure of my older siblings didn't make me any less invisible, but I was happy with being ignored at that point because things weren't going so well with Mom and Joe. There was a lot of drinking, and with the drinking came even more yelling around the house. There may have been only three of us at home now, but that didn't make my living situation any sweeter. More and more, I spent whatever free time I had outdoors.

There wasn't much wilderness in the suburban landscapes of Palatine and Libertyville, Illinois—two of the next stops on our family train—but I made do with what I could find. A backyard, a nearby park, a creek or a pond or a river—they all became sanctuaries of peace and predictability for me. I'd sit there for hours, watching the birds and the squirrels, lying in the grass and staring up at the clouds overhead, or just leaning up against a tree and observing. In those moments I felt like nobody could hurt me, that the world was a safe and welcoming place. I grew to appreciate the rhythm and predictability of the natural world. I realized that animals didn't do things out of spite; they didn't try to hurt one another just for the sake of it. They could be cunning and predatory, even deadly, but it was never personal. That's just how the natural world worked, and I found comfort in that consistency.

It wasn't until my mother sent me to a place called Fort Totten, North Dakota, to live with her friend Wynona in the summer between fifth and sixth grades that those feelings really began to blossom. Mom and I didn't talk much on the twelve-hour drive, but I'm sure that's how she wanted it. When I asked her why I had to spend the summer away, she said it was for my own good. I had no idea what that meant but didn't press her on it. Experience had shown me that when it came to sharing mundane details with me, my mother simply wasn't interested. (Years later, someone would joke that Fort Totten may have been where my biological dad lived. Whether that's true or not, I never found out. I could have passed him on the street and not known it at all.) So we sat there, silent but for the various radio stations that kept us company as we crossed from state to state. Meanwhile, I watched the world outside the car grow less populated with each mile, the landscapes wider, wilder, and, for me, increasingly enticing. When we finally arrived at Wynona's house, Mom spent the night, but she was gone before I woke up the next morning. I wouldn't talk to her until she came back for me six weeks later.

Fort Totten was a small place where everybody knew everybody else, a town within the Spirit Lake reservation where most people were of the Dakota tribe. The highlight of the town was the fort itself, a collection of stone and clapboard buildings set in a rectangle around a wide grassy courtyard that exuded a military gravity even my eleven-year-old self could appreciate. Perched high on a bluff, the view from the fort was spectacular, overlooking the wide blue expanse of Spirit Lake below. I may have been sent there to get out of my mother's hair, but my life in Illinois released its grip on my heart the first time I stood on that bluff. The green and golden hills in the distance rolled away to some great, wild unknown. Fort Totten was the most beautiful place I had ever been.

In my free time there—and I had *lots* of free time, as Wynona was busy working most days—I wandered around the gravel roads of the reservation and talked to people. Front doors were almost always unlocked, and people didn't seem to mind visitors. During my first week I knocked at the door of a modest white bungalow with an old pickup in the driveway, where a silver-haired man with dark, mysterious eyes and deep smile wrinkles at the corners of his eyes answered the door. "I'm Sue Moore," I said, thrusting my hand forward and shaking his in that exaggerated up-and-down way that kids do when they're trying to be polite. "I'm visiting here from Illinois for the summer."

“Why, hello there, Sue Moore who’s visiting here from Illinois for the summer.” He chuckled, the creases beside his eyes growing deeper in his dark skin. “Would you like a cup of tea?”

So began my relationship with Pat White, a Dakota elder who oozed a sense of peace, kindness, and quiet confidence that would resonate with me for the rest of my life. I was drawn to anybody who showed me kindness, but Pat White’s kindness was different. He exuded a deep wisdom that I’d never felt before. Mrs. McCaskey was loving, kind, and intelligent, but Pat White’s wisdom seemed to come from his bones or from the land and waters around the town he had called home his entire life. He probably wasn’t much past his sixties, but in some ways his lined and weathered face seemed as old as Spirit Lake itself.

I spent much of that summer in Pat’s company, whether we simply sat and drank tea on the flower-patterned couches in his living room or walked the gravel roads and green fields of the reservation. Like Mrs. McCaskey, Pat White didn’t merely tolerate me; he actually seemed to enjoy my company.

One morning, Pat and I wandered to the edge of the reservation past the old fort buildings, where the road ended and the wild began. The landscape stretched away before us forever, a rich mosaic of hills peppered with dense oak woodlands, mixed grass prairie, wetlands, and bands of wild horses alternately grazing, drinking, and trotting. My heart swelled. I realized this was the kind of place I wanted to be. Alone, with just the wind and the water and the trees and the animals spread across the hills. Pat stood still and quiet.

Then Pat made a series of sounds, a high-pitched trill followed by several short, sharp whistles, rhythmic lip smacks, and soft, gentle vocalizations similar to a horse's nicker. A band of horses about fifty yards away stopped their grazing and looked toward us. Then they started in our direction, at first a walk but soon a full trot. It was jarring to see that many powerful animals approaching me, but Pat never showed any sign of fear, and I tried to mimic his calmness as best I could. Soon the horses were all around us, Pat rubbing their necks and speaking softly to them in words I couldn't understand. For the first time in my life, I was in the company of kings.

Pat often took me out to the hills over the course of those six weeks. Whether he knew about my family history and felt some sense of obligation or simply enjoyed the company of an inquisitive girl from the suburbs of Chicago I'll never know. But I soaked up as much from him as I possibly could. During our walks I asked him questions about everything I saw.

"How do you snare an animal?" I asked. "How do you heal a wound? When do you know it's going to rain? Which plants can you eat? How can you find water?"

Pat answered every one of my questions the same way: slowly, patiently, and in detail. In fact, he taught me so much that I had to record it all to make sure I didn't forget a single thing. He gave me notebooks, which I filled with drawings, bits of plants, important things he had said. Recipes, edible flowers, medicine, plants and animals to stay away from, how to make soap, how to cook… I wrote it all down. I'd keep those journals with me for decades, until, in an errant fit of necessity and shortsightedness, I married a man I had no business marrying and he took them when he left me high and dry in the Alaskan winter.

Pat and I often came across the horses on our adventures. Every time we did, he made that same collection of sounds, and the horses would trot over to where we were standing. Eventually, he taught me how to do it too. As hard as I tried, though, I could never get them to approach.

"You keep trying, Susie," he said gently, putting his hand on my shoulder as I hung my head in disappointment. "You'll get it eventually. But remember that you have to earn their trust. I see that you're always going to be alone in this life, Susie. The animals are going to be your guides, not the people. So you better get used to it, and you better always say thanks."

On the morning of the day my mother was coming to pick me up, Pat took me out for one final exploration of the land beyond the edge of town. The wild horses were scattered across the hills, just like they'd been every morning. Once again, I called them the way Pat taught me.

This time, though, they came.

Back at home, it was as if Fort Totten had never happened. There was a palpable tension between my mother and Joe, and the drinking and yelling were worse than before I had left. I spent as much time as I could outside, trying desperately to hold on to the memories of Pat White and the things he had taught me. I took my notebooks to the parks and the ponds and the rivers and wrote down everything I saw and did. Pat was gone from my life, but those books kept me connected to him, and I held on to them for dear life.

One night, a few days before school started up again, I was asleep in bed when Mom came into my room. “Hey!” she whispered huskily with a sense of urgency that startled me. “Hey!” she said again. “Wake up!”

I had no idea what time it was but could tell it was either the middle of the night or ridiculously early in the morning because it was still dark outside. I wiped my eyes and peered at her through the dark. She was holding an empty paper grocery bag. “Here,” she said, pushing the bag into my hands. “Pack this. We’re going.”

“OK,” I mumbled. I should otherwise have been utterly confused by what was happening in my room in the middle of the night, but nothing in my life surprised me anymore; I took it as it came. Still, this was out of the ordinary even for my out-of-the-ordinary life. “Where are we going?” I asked as I stuffed some clothes and my notebooks into the bag.

“We’re moving to Alaska.”

The next morning, we did.

The driving distance between Palatine, Illinois, and the town of Prince Rupert, Canada, is roughly 2,500 miles, depending on which route you take. If you do it straight, you could knock out the trip in forty hours, but it took Mom and me and our Chevy Suburban a couple of weeks. That's a long time to not speak, and there were many long and lonely parts of the road where we couldn't get any stations on the radio, so my mother eventually caved in and talked to me from time to time. Not about anything important or meaningful, mind you—I was still not important enough to be worthy of such details—but at least there was something to break up the silence.

Some parts of the trip were full of wonder. I looked out the window longingly at the lands speeding past, wild and open places where a girl could get lost and never found. We pitched our Coleman tent in whatever campground we could find, and when we couldn't find one, we slept in the Suburban. As confused as I was about what was happening and as uncomfortable as it was being with my mother day and night, I relished the time we spent outdoors. Sometimes I'd slip out in the middle of the night and look up at the stars. If I stood there quietly for long enough, the forest would eventually return to life around me, the *woo-hoo* of an owl in a tree overhead, the unmistakable sound of tiny paws walking through the leaves. On some nights, coyotes yipped far off in the distance, an eerie sound that kept me rooted to my spot in fear and wonder.

We continued that way for days, occasionally stopping to see the sights, breaking down, waiting for repairs, and then moving on again. *Wait… Are we on vacation?* I asked at one point. *No. Get back in the car; let's go.* Through it all, although Mom and I were always together, we were never present with one another. We never discussed the reason for our journey. It's like a cake—you can see the frosting, but the flavor remains a mystery until you take the first bite. But I hadn't been given a fork.

From Prince Rupert, a picturesque coastal city in British Columbia surrounded by rugged rainforest, a ferry took us north to Anchorage, Alaska. Luckily the ship afforded Mom and me much-needed distance from one another. I stood on the highest deck and watched the world float by: mysterious islands shrouded in fog, ancient forests holding untold secrets. Eagles soared overhead, whales breached in the waters around us. I may have been alone, confused, and scared, but seeing those things somehow grounded me. I was thousands of miles away from home…and yet I somehow felt like I was exactly where I was meant to be.

From Anchorage we drove the final 350 miles north to Fairbanks. And even though we were clearly getting closer to our final destination, we never discussed the future. If there was a big plan, I was never privy to it. The only details I'd been given were that my brother Charlie was living or homesteading somewhere near Fairbanks and that we were going to stay on or near his property. Destination notwithstanding, I couldn't shake the feeling that a hammer was about to fall, only I didn't know how or when or why.

Finally, we arrived. A patch in the woods off a gravel road in the middle of nowhere. Mom never told me what happened with Joe or what drove her to leave the life she knew in Illinois to move three thousand miles away. Information only came on a need-to-know basis, and as always, I didn't need to know. Didn't matter. It was history. We were there, and I would do what I'd always done: look for the rainbow in the storm.

Charlie's property—which was located about fifty miles outside Fairbanks—didn't turn out to be what I thought. Instead of the rustic log cabin in the woods I was expecting, it was just woods, a piece of land indistinguishable from the sweeping landscape of trees around it. He also owned a second piece of land on the same road, one Mom had pointed out when we passed it, but for some reason she thought this one suited us better.

Once we settled in and set up camp, nothing much was different than our stops along the way; it was just the two of us in the tent, minus the driving. Charlie wasn't there when we arrived, apparently working somewhere farther north on the Alaskan pipeline.

So there we were, shoved into unfamiliar terrain in one of the most formidable places on the planet, not knowing a single person around us except a brother who was nowhere to be found. I'd noticed a few rough-looking buildings and cabins on the drive to our final camping spot, which I assumed were populated with crazy, gun-totin', white-bearded bushmen who were either searching for gold in nearby rivers or running from the law.

From the few details I was able to get from my mother, I gathered that we were now living off a long stretch of gravel road that ran between Fairbanks and a place called Chena Hot Springs. The Chena Hot Springs Road, she called it. There were no addresses; people simply shared their location by how far they were along the road from Fairbanks. *Old Bobby Sue? She lives at 30 mile. Billy Jack is at 44 mile.*

We stopped in Fairbanks once for groceries, before our final push out to the campsite we called home. We didn't walk around much, but I liked what I saw. The town exuded a rugged, independent frontier spirit that was evident everywhere you looked. Old, colorful buildings with porches and hand-painted signs lined the streets where roughshod miners in overalls walked beside native Alaskans who reminded me of Pat White. A crystal clear river (which I'd later learn was the Chena River) ran through the heart of downtown; beyond it a series of hills rolled into rugged, snowcapped mountains and the broadest expanse of forest and wilderness I'd ever seen.

And while my physical surroundings and the circumstances of my life had changed, other things remained predictably consistent, particularly when it came to my mother. One evening, I spent nearly an hour gathering kindling, stacking the twigs neatly into a tepee, and then striking the matches with growing frustration as the wind kept snuffing them out. When the fire finally caught, I stepped back proudly, only to have her shake her head and remind me that my fire wasn't much of one at all. Undaunted, three nights later I decided to surprise her by making dinner while she rested. I carefully boiled pasta on the camp stove, stirred in canned tomato sauce, and even sprinkled some grated cheese on top, just like I'd once seen in a cookbook. When I handed her the bowl, though, she barely took a bite before wrinkling her nose and telling me how bland it was.

None of this came as a surprise; I had grown accustomed to not being good enough. But over the years, I had come up with a defense mechanism for her constant belittling. Rather than get bogged down in the pain that accompanied emotional challenges, I instead opted to treat them logically and systematically, assimilating them into my brain and then deciding if a reaction would effect positive change. If the answer was "no," then I simply chose to accept the pattern of behavior and move on. It doesn't mean I necessarily *liked* what was happening to me, but at least I could live with it. Maybe that's why they say I have the emotional development of a child; I stopped dealing with feelings a long time ago. For the rest of my life, I wouldn't really know what to do with emotions. I feel them, but I don't process them very well. And if I hold them too long, I am consumed by them. So I either file them away or forget about them.

My mother otherwise spent the first two weeks of our time in the woods as if it were a vacation, sitting in a chair or lying in a hammock reading. I passed my days exploring, at first to simply create space between us. But over the course of those two weeks, something miraculous happened. I stopped feeling sorry for myself and started appreciating the land around me, a land as untamed and untrammeled as any, the biggest playground a child of Earth could hope to discover.

At first I saw our small patch of Alaska merely as a forest thick with black and white spruce, aspen, and birch trees. As I grew bolder, I began to explore in ever-widening circles around camp, soon discovering lush valleys pierced by clear and free-flowing rivers and creeks framed by green-carpeted hills reaching up toward gentle mountains overhead. Sometimes I'd stumble into open meadows abuzz with bees as wildflowers bloomed riotously all around me. Eventually, I became a part of the landscape, not just a visitor. I was alone and ignored, but somehow I was home.

Then, on an afternoon of a day much like the others, Mom started putting on her coat and shoes.

"What are you doing?" I asked.

"Running into town for a few things."

"Can I come with?"

"No," she said flatly. Then she softened. "But I'll get you something. What do you want?"

I'd lived with that woman long enough to know when something was wrong, and something was *definitely* wrong. Rare were the times that she offered to buy me anything. I couldn't reply.

And that was the end of the conversation. She went inside the tent, grabbed the truck keys. She seemed to be in a hurry; I didn't ask why. I watched her walk away, but she didn't look back, didn't wave, didn't say goodbye. Moments later there was a churn of gravel and she was gone.

She didn't buy me anything.

She didn't come back at all that day or that night, either.

In fact, she didn't come back at all.

The next morning I woke up in the tent and looked for her beside me, but she wasn't there. I didn't want to admit it, but a part of me wished something had happened to my mother. Truck went off the road and plunged into the river. Hit a moose and was lying unconscious in a ditch. Not because I actually wanted her to be hurt… but if something had happened, at least that meant she didn't just leave me.

How old was I? Young enough that it hurt. Despite everything I had tried to teach myself about girding my heart against the disappointment and the barbs, it still hurt. I know more of the story now but didn't then. So back in that campsite in Alaska, the twelve-year-old me held on to the ten-year-old me, the five-year-old me, and the two-year-old me and tried to offer some semblance of comfort. It wasn't easy. My mother went to town and didn't come back.

I was alone. It's a feeling that would remain with me in some form for years to come: the fear of being completely and totally forgettable. And yet I hate that I ever gave someone that power over me. I would feel for many years that I was not enough until I came to realize that enough is all I am.

I wanted to tell myself that she would come back. I wanted to tell myself she would never do something like that to me. I didn't know if she loved me, didn't know if she ever had. But still, she would definitely come back for me, wouldn't she?

The hours blurred together into a mass of forgetfulness. Morning turned to afternoon turned to night. Night turned to day. I collapsed on the ground outside the tent and slept there, just so I could hear the truck coming down the road. I lost sense of time after the first day, and then I started to lose sense of space and reality. I cried. I screamed. I raged. Even at night when the darkness surrounded me, every sound was a possibility.

"Mom?" I said. No answer.

By the third morning, reality began to set in. Slowly and imperceptibly, I began to change directions in my head. The thoughts of hurt and desperation began to diminish slightly, replaced by another, stronger one.

She's not coming back. Shit.

She's not coming back. Maybe…just wait.

She's not coming back. Now what?

At that same moment, a raven landed on the ground not far from where I was lying. I turned on my side to face it and its thick, gnarled beak, piercing black eyes like an abyss.

"What do you want?" I yelled.

The raven studied me, head cocked to one side, and then hopped a little closer.

"WHAT DO YOU WANT?" I screamed louder.

Again the raven hopped closer, now only a couple feet from my face. I didn't move. I didn't care.

"What?" I screamed. "Go ahead and peck my eyes out! Go ahead, do it. Everybody hates me anyway! Nobody ever wanted me. Just. Fucking. Do. It!"

I was screaming as loud as I could, but the stupid bird refused to fly away. The raven cocked its head again, looking at me with one eye. It hopped closer again. One foot away now. Maybe it was deciding what part of me to peck first. Hop. Closer. Hop hop. Only inches away. I figured it would go for my eyes first, but I didn't close them. *Go ahead and do it*, I thought. *Now I'll be Little Susie Blind Girl, the abandoned girl of Alaska.* Then it happened.

Head still cocked, marble-black eyeball locked onto mine, impervious to my screams, the raven lowered its glossy blue-back head and pushed it into my chest. One long wing extended up and out and then came to a rest on my side. It's crazy, I know, and I'm crazy for believing it because to this day I wonder if it actually happened or if I was merely hallucinating. But in my mind, it happened as palpably as anything has ever happened to me. The raven was *hugging* me. For a brief moment, I had a vision of standing on the hills with Pat White and calling to the horses.

I froze, but not out of fear. I froze because in that single moment in time, I felt loved. I am crazy for thinking it and maybe even crazier for feeling it. But I did. The raven saw me, appreciated me, perhaps even loved me. I lifted my arm, and as best I could, I hugged it back. The raven hopped away and looked at me once again.

"Hi, George," I said.

Then, without warning, all the emotions I'd bottled up inside for the past few days—maybe for the past many years—exploded out of me like a geyser. I didn't hold back. All the anger, fear, betrayal, and rejection I'd been holding on to came raging out of me into the afternoon air. And through it all, George looked on, head still cocked as I cried and wailed. Then, just like that, it was over. I was purged.

"Right," I said to George, myself, and anyone or anything else close enough to hear. "This isn't going to change. Mom's onto a new life and isn't coming back, so I better get on with mine."

Is it shitty that life tossed me to the wolves? Maybe. It's not how I would have scripted my own story, but it made me who

I am. And now, I finally had a chance to be free of the nightly screaming, the relentless anxiety. I'd had my cry with George, but it was done.

I stood up and brushed myself off.

"All right," I said to Sue and George at the same time. "Let's do this."

CHAPTER 2

THE WILD CHILD

The first order of business was to get something in my stomach. I hadn't eaten in days, and after I pulled myself off the forest floor, my appetite came roaring back with a fury. Luckily my mother hadn't taken the food, so I stuffed myself full of as many bologna and mayonnaise sandwiches and Fritos as I could manage. George watched me warily from a few yards away, greedily gobbling up whatever scraps I tossed him. When both our bellies seemed full, it was time to decide my next course of action.

I turned the options over in my mind, though there weren't many. I could walk down the Chena Hot Springs Road to seek help at the nearest cabin, but the thought of coming face-to-face with whatever crazy, white-bearded miner or hardened criminal who undoubtedly lived inside was not comforting. Maybe I would find assistance, but maybe I would find something much, much worse. Plus, a part of me held out hope that my mother would eventually return, and I didn't want to alert anyone to her disappearance for fear that it might get her into some kind of trouble with the law. For all the challenging, difficult, and downright cruel things she had done to me up to that point in my life, I still loved my mother very much and didn't want to see her hurt.

So I decided to walk, with no apparent destination in mind. In the weeks I'd lived in Alaska, I'd fallen in love with the land, and once I got over the pain of being abandoned, I realized that my fate wasn't as horrible as I had originally thought. I was in the most beautiful place I had ever seen, surrounded by trees and plants and birds and animals that accepted me, and I didn't have anybody telling me what to do or how to do it. Things could have been much worse.

Buoyed by those thoughts, I grabbed my mother's backpack and stuffed it full of as many useful items as I could find in our camp. In went the Swiss Army knife, a thermos, a Tupperware plate and cup, a few utensils. In went my sleeping bag and clothes, the flashlight, the lighter and matches, and the Band-Aids. Finally, in went whatever food I could squeeze into the space that remained. And in my hands went the notebooks I had meticulously compiled during my time with Pat White.

The only thing I knew at that point was that Fairbanks was to the left. Turning left likely meant returning to *society*, a world that had consistently let me down. I may have been thousands of miles from Illinois, but people were people, and in the end I wanted to avoid them. To the right was the yellow brick road, a path of mystery and possibility, where nobody would decide what happened to me but *me*. To the left was my past; to the right my future.

I took one last look around the camp that had been my home for the past two and a half weeks and then took a deep breath and walked to the edge of the road. "Bye, George," I said. And then I turned right.

Though it's much busier now, there was very little traffic on the road in those days, which suited me just fine. I simply didn't want to be found. On the few occasions that I heard tires churning up the gravel from a long way away, I ducked down into the trees and bushes and made myself scarce. I know I should have been terrified—I was a twelve-year-old girl alone in Alaska—but I wasn't. And with each step I took toward a destination I could not see, I grew a little bit bolder. In those moments that doubt began to creep into my mind, I kept telling myself the same thing over and over again: *You'll figure it out. One step at a time. You'll figure it out.*

My lessons with Pat White were still fresh in my mind, the tips and tricks he had taught me about the land and living in harmony with it, and I was eager to put them to use. I found comfort in knowing that my notebooks were right there with me. It was almost as if Pat were with me too. But he wasn't the only one who had taught me how to fend for myself.

My great-grandmother on my mother's side was Ma Binnie, a stout, silver-haired firecracker of a Scottish woman who emanated a formidable, old-world independence I'd never encountered until I met her for the first time on a family visit to her house in Fort Atkinson, Wisconsin, when I was eight. From the moment I was introduced to Ma Binnie, I was enthralled. It didn't take long to recognize two very important characteristics that defined Ma. First, she knew how to handle herself in almost any situation: If something needed to get done, Ma did it. You got the feeling from Ma that she could be dropped anywhere on Earth and would still be able to carve out a life for herself. Second, Ma didn't take shit from anyone. I liked that about her too.

That first evening in Fort Atkinson, I was alone in the kitchen with Ma while she made dinner: rabbit and spaghetti using rabbits she had shot, skinned, and butchered in the fields near her house. I stood in a corner of the kitchen, watching with rapt attention as her strong, wrinkled hands moved deftly from task to task, slicing meat, chopping vegetables, and stirring the big pots on the stovetop.

Ma caught sight of me. "What do yeh think yer doin'?" she asked, turning to face me and wiping her hands on her apron.

"Watching you cook. I want to cook like you do."

"You're a nosy wee lass."

"I want to learn," I said. If I were going to be a self-sufficient ass-kicker like Ma, I needed to know how to do the same things she did.

Ma peered at me over her glasses. "Listen here," she said in an accent so thick I could barely understand her. "You're nay a real woman if yeh dinna know how tae cook. Understan? Yeh got to do it yourself—*by hand*—or you're neh a woman."

By her own definition, Ma was *definitely* a woman. She did everything by hand. We would visit her a few times over the next couple of years, and every time we did, I learned a little bit more about my incredibly capable great-grandmother. She ate the meat of the animals she hunted and snared. In the fall, she canned the fruit and vegetables she grew all summer. Her bread was homemade; she sewed most of the clothes on her back. And if anyone was feeling sick, they were subjected to heavy doses of Ma's handcrafted medicines, a collection of pastes and syrups and salves that smelled like death but worked like hell.

I know this because I once made the mistake of admitting to her that I had a cold. Ma was on me in an instant, wiping me down with some foul-looking goop she pulled out of a jar in the pantry. "What the hell?" I cried. "Stop!"

"Sit down, yeh wee snipe," she said, her thick hands pushing me down onto a chair. "You're going to put this all over yeh…and you're going to *heal*." Arguing with Ma was futile, so I stopped wriggling and held my breath as she dipped two fingers into the jar and spread the salve on my neck and chest. I couldn't stand my own stench as I lay in bed that night, but when morning came, I'll be damned if I didn't feel better. We drove away from Ma's house that morning the same way we did every time, with her standing on the porch waving with one hand and the other firmly planted on her ample hip. *That*, I thought, *is the kind of woman you want to be.*

I held visions of both Pat White and Ma in my mind as I walked. They were my protectors, my guides. They would figure out how to survive and get on with it. They'd hunt their food, snare it, grow it, or gather it. They'd make their own clothes, if they had to.

It didn't take long before my steps took on a rhythmic, almost meditative nature. I was no longer an outsider on a gravel strip in an unknown land but just another animal living its life. I lost track of time, alternating between walking and stopping to eat and rest. I knew the food in my pack wouldn't last very long, so I ate what the land provided whenever I could. Mostly I feasted on the berries that burst forth from the bushes in the short Alaskan summer. When there were none to be found, I resorted to eating other things Pat had shown me, like the leaves and inner bark of willow bushes, which he said had medicinal properties like aspirin. Fireweed flowers and leaves were plentiful and tasty, as long as they hadn't gone cottony.

The silence wrapped me in its arms as I walked. Other than my breathing and the crunch of gravel under my feet, there were few other man-made sounds. Then, when I ducked off the road to rest, the forest came to life around me. Pat taught me that nature is a symphony of sound, if you just take the time to listen. When I got tired at day's end, I found a sheltered space in the woods, unrolled my sleeping bag, and fell asleep instantly, surprisingly at peace with my circumstances.

On my second day out, I passed a milepost marker: mile 48. I was forty-eight miles from Fairbanks, though anything resembling the outside world seemed a million miles away. How long would I walk? I had no idea. *One step at a time. You'll figure it out.* The signs said I was getting closer to a place called Chena Hot Springs, but I wasn't sure I was ready to be in the company of the people I assumed I'd find there. Later that afternoon, as I stopped to load up on a patch of wild raspberries, I looked up to see a large black raven looking down at me from a branch overhead.

"Hi, George," I said. I had no idea if it was the same bird that had embraced me back in camp, but it didn't matter. Every raven was George, *my* George. For the rest of my days, every raven that entered my life would forever be known as George.

The road grew hillier as I walked, steadily gaining elevation. On either side of me, the woods, once thick with spruce trees, began to open up. To my left, those clearings—thick with patches of willows, dwarf birch, and berry bushes of every shape and color—revealed vistas of hills and ridgetops rolling back toward distant mountain ranges.

Later that afternoon, I noticed a trail bending off the road and through the trees on my left. I'd passed other trails diverging from the road on my walk, but this one spoke to me like the others hadn't, and I decided to follow. The path wound its way through the trees, diving ever deeper into the woods toward the hills beyond. It was overgrown with bushes and crisscrossed with fallen timber and looked like it hadn't been used in years, if not decades, but I followed it nonetheless. Not far ahead I could hear the sound of running water, and as I got closer, all signs of the road behind me disappeared.

A few minutes later, the trail spit me out into a clearing, on the far side of which flowed the river. I'd later learn that it was the North Fork Chena River, one of the two primary tributaries that feed the mighty Chena River itself. Not far from its bank sat a small, rundown, yet pretty-as-a-picture cabin. The cabin had clearly been neglected for a very long time, but with the sun filtering through the leaves and the fireweed dancing in the breeze, I didn't see a single imperfection. Like me, the cabin seemed forgotten and alone but loaded with potential.

I was intrigued but wary. Although the cabin looked abandoned, there was still a good chance it housed that crazy, white-bearded miner or miscreant I'd conjured in my imagination, so I ducked behind a tree and watched. It was difficult to hear anything above the rush of the river, but a half hour of observation convinced me I was alone. There was no evidence of recent human activity anywhere outside the cabin, no footprints, no sign of a fire, no vehicle tracks… nothing that time and nature hadn't deposited there.

With dusk falling, I emerged from my spot in the trees and approached the cabin. Up close, I could see in detail how rough it was: Its low roof was covered in moss and branches and caved in on one side, one of its two little windows broken. The wooden front door was hanging sickly off its hinges in the frame, and when I slid past it, I could see that the musty interior was littered with signs of animals.

It was perfect.

That cabin—that tiny, rundown, forgotten, hidden cabin—was my little piece of heaven. It had clearly not been inhabited for many years and in more than a few places was literally falling apart. But the log walls were thick and solid, and the river—a source of fresh water and maybe even food—was just a few feet away. I knew the cabin wasn't mine and figured anybody could show up at any time and kick me out, but for the time being it was home.

Home. I dropped my backpack and set about to cleaning the place. As I did, I realized the cabin had been built a long time before: Whoever stayed there had apparently carved their name or initials into the logs inside, along with the years they stayed there. The oldest one I found made me feel very small in the world, indeed: *J. W. 1852.* Decades later I would learn that the cabin was one of several satellite houses built by the family that settled the area when they ultimately "discovered" Chena Hot Springs. Since then it had been used intermittently by the family, along with a host of hodgepodge of trappers and loners. But in that moment, there by myself in the glorious days of an Alaskan summer, it was all mine.

I passed the weeks lazily and felt carefree in a way I'd rarely felt to that point in my life, unburdened by the weight of expectation or the sense that I was an ongoing disappointment to the world. By day, I explored the land around the cabin, basked in the warmth of the sun at the river's edge, and made my new home as livable as possible. The woods and fields around the cabin were positively bursting with berries, and after I finished the food I'd taken from camp, I fed myself almost exclusively on those.

Years later I would realize that as wonderful as the entire state of Alaska is for berry picking in the summer, the area around what I'll come to call "the Chena cabin" is, serendipitously enough, as spectacular as it gets: salmon berries, blueberries, crowberries, strawberries, raspberries, gooseberries, high- and low-bush cranberries. If there is a singular sensation I'll come to associate with my time at the cabin, it will be the rich aroma of those high-bush cranberries filling the air. And yet, as the days wound on, I knew they wouldn't last forever; already the nights were getting cooler and longer. Soon my primary food source would disappear completely.

A few weeks into my stay, I was wandering through my favorite berry patch, the bees buzzing lazily around me. Between stuffing cranberries into my mouth and filling the rusted Maxwell House coffee tin I'd found in the cabin, I called out and sang to whatever animal was close enough to hear. I had yet to run into anything larger than a fox, but the signs of big game were never far away. Piles of bear scat were common on the game trails around the cabin, and in the muddy low-lying areas I often saw moose tracks and the flattened grass where they'd slept not long before. For some reason, though, the knowledge that I was sharing the woods with creatures much bigger and wilder than me had me wary but not terrified. The way I saw it, we were all living a grand adventure together.

My can full, my hands stained, and my appetite quelled, I walked back toward the cabin. Somewhere deep in my consciousness I knew I should be making noise as I walked, but in that moment the magic of the wild was so profound that I couldn't think of anything else. Oblivious to everything else around me, I broke through a stand of trees, and ten feet in front of me was a massive black bear, fat with the richness of summer, its coat shining in the sun.

For a moment we stared wide-eyed at one another. Then I let out a scream, dropped the can on the ground, turned, and sprinted back down the trail. I've since learned enough about bears to recognize it was the worst thing I could have done (running often triggers a predatory response in an otherwise placid bear), but survival instinct is an irresistible force, and in that moment my survival instinct was deafening: *Run!*

Meanwhile, the bear let out a primal roar of its own behind me, a sound that reminded me of Joe stubbing his toe on a coffee table in the middle of the night. I was certain my life was about to come to a brutish end, but when I turned around, all I saw was the bear loping off in the opposite direction, its fat-laden skin undulating across its body in waves.

Life at the Chena cabin continued with much the same rhythm for the next two months. By late September, the only berries left in the area were the crowberries, which seemed even sweeter after an evening frost, which now happened on most mornings. Soon even the crowberries were gone, though, leaving me anxious to find other sources of food. The river was thick with fish, but I couldn't entice any of them to bite the paper clip I'd tied to the fishing line I'd found in the cabin.

With little other choice, I got creative. After a frustrating amount of trial and error, I eventually figured out that if I built a good enough diversion out of rocks, I could trap the occasional grayling in a pool and spear it with a sharpened stick. Once I found a moose carcass in the woods. It was crawling in maggots, but I knew the meat could sustain me for a long time, so did my best to numb my senses and override the feelings of disgust that welled up as I considered the rank meat. I breathed through my mouth as I picked the maggots off, shallow breaths that somehow kept the smell from overwhelming me. Later, as I cooked the meat over a fire, I forced myself to go numb and compartmentalize the task at hand. I wasn't eating rotting flesh, I was taking charge of my own survival. All things considered, I was rarely hungry.

As much as I loved my life at the cabin, though, I began to realize that my time there was coming to a rapid end with the coming winter. The sum total of my Alaskan experience had been limited to a couple of months, but I knew enough that I wouldn't survive the winter alone there. At the same time, I also began to think about my future. If I was truly destined to be on my own, then I was eventually going to have to get a job. And if I wanted any kind of decent job, then I needed to get back to school and get done with it as quickly as possible. It was time to go. But where?

As I pondered the question, I remembered that my brother Charlie owned another property on the Chena road, the one closer to Fairbanks that my mother had pointed out when we first passed it on our drive here. Its exact location was a mystery, but the road only went two ways, and I knew it was toward Fairbanks. How difficult could it be? *One step at a time. You'll figure it out.*

With a heavy heart, I bade farewell to the Chena cabin, but not before I carved my name into one of its logs. Then I walked back toward the road and turned right.

As I had the first time, I kept to myself as I walked. The next morning I reached the spot where Mom and I had camped. Everything was in the same place I'd left it when I'd walked away, except the animals had clearly picked through the little bit of food I'd left behind. I took a quick look around for signs of my mother, and when I realized she hadn't returned, I continued on, more determined than ever to get on with my life. At the same time, though, I knew I couldn't be solitary forever; eventually I was going to have to interact with people so they could help me figure out how to find my eldest brother.

On the third day out, I came across a narrow drive through the trees on my left and turned to follow it. The drive eventually opened into a clearing peppered with a jumble of buildings: single trailers married up with double-wides somehow attached to barn-type structures. Alabama meets Alaska. There were kids playing outside, some barefoot, all dirty and unkempt. They eyed me warily as I knocked on the front door, but I figured I was getting closer to Charlie's property and it was time to ask for directions.

"What do you want?" a woman asked, looking at me through the narrow crack in the door.

"I'm looking for a man named Charlie Moore; I think he has property out this way," I said.

"You alone?" she asked.

"Yep."

"Wait here," the woman replied, and closed the door. A minute later she appeared from around the back of the trailer, with a baby on her hip and accompanied by a man. He eyed me with the same wary look his children had given me. "I hear you're looking for Charlie Moore's place," he said.

"I am. I'm his sister." The man seemed to soften a bit. The twelve-year-old girl before him was clearly not a threat.

"I'm Rick Powalski, and this here is Jan," he said, indicating his wife. "Charlie's land is just down the road a ways. Jan will show you where it is." Jan handed the baby to Rick and led me to the truck. "You know Charlie's not there, right?" Rick called out after us. "Been working up on the oil fields for months and isn't likely to come back anytime soon."

We drove in silence for a couple of minutes, the truck bumping along the road when Jan said, "You lookin' for work?" I hesitated, if only because I doubted the work she'd have would be particularly wholesome and fulfilling. But work was work and nobody else was offering any.

"I guess," I answered warily.

"What do you think about babysitting our kids during the days while we're working?" she asked. "We'll pay you, and you can eat with us while you're at the house." It was a tempting offer, particularly the food part. With most of the berries gone, I'd eaten little over the past few days, and my hunger was palpable. Yet at the same time, I realized the Powalskis probably had few other options for childcare in the middle of the Chena road, so I took the opportunity to ask for the thing I wanted most of all.

"OK," I said. "But I need you to do something for me too. I want to go to school and need someone to enroll me." Jan considered me for a second as she turned left on a smaller track a mile or so from their place and then stuck out her hand to shake mine. "You got a deal." Not long after, she stopped the truck.

"This is it," she said. "Not sure what you're looking for, but this is Charlie Moore's property." I grabbed the backpack and my journals and hopped out. As she turned the truck around, she leaned out the window. "Come by in the morning." Then she was gone in a cloud of dust.

Charlie's land didn't seem any different from his other property, though the rough beginnings of a small cabin showed that maybe he intended to live there at some point. Since Charlie was thirteen years older than me, I'd had very little to do with him in Illinois, and I had no idea if he'd welcome me into his life…or if I wanted him in mine. For the time being, knowing the location of his property was good enough. I shouldered the bag and walked down the dirt road a ways until another track, forgotten and overgrown, opened up on my right.

I followed the track, which eventually ended at a small clearing in the trees. It looked like somebody had once considered building here, but the idea must have faded in the backdrop of another million Alaskan dreams, and the wild was slowly reclaiming the space, with bushes and saplings now crowding the building site.

It wasn't my little cabin but seemed as good a spot as any to hang my hat until I found more permanent shelter. I set down my pack, unrolled my sleeping bag, and fell fast asleep on the downy turf.

The next morning I walked to the Powalskis and spent the day watching their kids. And the next and the next after that. At the end of my third day, Jan said, "Where are you sleeping?"

"In my sleeping bag."

"That's it?" she asked. "Just a sleeping bag on the ground?"

"Yep."

She looked at me with a mix of wonder and pity. "I want to show you something," she said. "Come with me." Soon we were driving down the same dirt road that led past Charlie's property and my clearing. A little father along we crossed a one-lane bridge over the Chena River, when Jan stopped.

"This is the dump at the Fort Wainwright army base," she said. "They throw away the best stuff; some of it's near new."

The dump was a gift from the heavens, the lifeline I needed to get me through the impending Alaskan winter. I scavenged a pair of winter boots, a parka, and other warm but ill-fitting clothes. But the biggest score of all was an eleven-foot-by-eleven-foot canvas wall tent, which we put in the back of the truck and drove back to my clearing. "If you get real lucky, you might even find a wood stove," Jan said as she drove away. I spent the next two evenings after work erecting the tent into shape using spruce poles I gathered from the forest. And like Jan had predicted, my trips to the dump bore fruit a few weeks later when I found an M-1941 tent stove and dragged it the couple of miles back to my tent.

Meanwhile, the Powalskis continued to feed me and pay me, offering me a sense of independence I hadn't known before. Cash in hand, I occasionally hitched a ride for the twenty-mile trip into Fairbanks, where I bought food and supplies. The first few times I searched for my mother in every person I passed on the street, but with time I stopped looking. I don't think she would have recognized me anyway. No longer was I the insecure, awkward kid who had driven across the country with her from Illinois. With each passing day, I was starting to believe I could survive by my own wits and skills. Ma Binnie and Pat White would've been proud.

In time, I started to see my mother and the circumstances of my life in a different light. It would have been easy to hate her, but I had no interest in holding on to feelings that would only drag me down. Life sucked sometimes. *My* life sucked sometimes. But at the same time, life was often brilliant and always had the potential to get better. So I chose to focus on *that* reality. For the rest of my life, I'd carry that flame of hope inside me, just as I did on those trips into Fairbanks, where the only thing I wished for my mother was happiness. I know now what I was starting to recognize then: It's all too easy to get mired in the tragedy of life. But if we only focus on what's wrong, we'll never see what's right.

A couple of weeks later, I was officially enrolled in school. As Jan told me later, the process was Alaskan easy, meaning nobody really cared enough to ask more than a few cursory questions.

"Where are the kid's parents?" the woman at the school asked.

"Not in town," Jan said. "Her brother's her guardian now, but he's Upslope working. He'll come in to sign everything when he gets back."

"Good enough for me." And that, apparently, was that.

Jan showed me the spot on the Chena road where the bus would pick me up, and the next day I walked into the North Pole School, in North Pole, Alaska, for the first time. With no history to document my educational progress to that point, I needed to be tested to determine what grade I'd be in. I thought it strange, but apparently it was common practice in the area, where most of the so-called "remote kids" had backgrounds as mysterious as mine.

I took one test, then another and another. After a full morning of testing, a woman with glasses sat down with me. "Well, dear," she said. "We've given you the year-end exams for sixth, seventh, and eighth grade, and you passed every one. I'm not sure this is the best idea, but it seems you're going into ninth grade."

Months passed. I did well in school but kept a low profile for fear that somebody would learn about my living situation and try to throw me into foster care. In time, though, I realized that living outside the box of conventional society was normal in Alaska in the 1970s. The only person other than the Powalskis who knew about my situation was my bus driver, Carl, a longtime Alaskan who had spent decades carving out a life for himself and his family until he decided to spend his twilight years in the relative relaxation of a rattletrap school bus bumping along a gravel road twice a day. Like Pat White and Ma before him, Carl soon became a source of knowledge for me.

Carl's bus traveled the sixty-odd miles from Fairbanks all the way out to the Chena Hot Springs, where it turned around and made its way back to North Pole, picking up kids along the way. I soon realized that if I got out to the road early enough, Carl would pick me up on the way out to Chena, leaving us more than an hour to chat by ourselves.

Each morning I posed an encyclopedia of questions to Carl, and he never seemed to tire of them. In those rare moments when he wasn't burdened by another one of my endless queries, Carl told me stories about life in Alaska, about the history of the area, about what to do and what not to do to survive. Those talks would become some of the best memories of my youth.

Yet in all those conversations, Carl never addressed my living situation with me. It was the Alaskan way. People mostly lived there because they wanted to be free of the constraints that accompanied life in the Lower 48. They were the free spirits and the rebels, the hippies and the reprobates. And if a teenage girl was living by herself in a canvas tent, well then, so be it. At the same time, Carl also knew that surviving an Alaskan winter was no game.

One morning he stopped to pick me up, and as soon as I sat down, he handed me a rifle. "Listen, kid," he said. "I don't know what's going on in your life, but I figure this is going to come in real handy." Then he took the gun back and stashed it in a rifle bag under his seat and said, "Starting this afternoon, I'm gonna teach you how to hunt."

That afternoon I stayed on past my stop and rode all the way out toward the hot springs with Carl, where he parked the empty bus. After walking through the woods for a bit, we entered a clearing, where he had set up a variety of targets. "OK, kid," he said, picking up the rifle. "See that can over there?" He shouldered the gun and fired, and the can disappeared from its perch. "Now you try."

Carl took me shooting after school almost every day for the next week. When we weren't shooting, he taught me about hunting. How to track an animal. Where to shoot it for a clean kill. Firearm safety. How to gut and skin an animal, from a rabbit to a deer to a bear. Eventually his lessons started to sink in and I began to feel more confident with the weapon in my hands. Soon I was crossing the bridge onto the army base, where I set up targets and shot at them myself. Ten yards away. Then twenty-five. In time, I began to hit them more regularly.

With spring approaching, I shot a deer. It was the first animal I'd ever killed, and the act affected me deeply. I knew I needed to eat and the deer would provide me with enough meat to last a long time, especially if I smoked it. But as I watched the life ebb from its eyes, I realized that when you were living on your own in Alaska, life and death were very closely connected. Sometimes, I decided, it was hard to tell them apart.

When nature didn't provide, I had to turn to other food sources. I was still babysitting for the Powalskis on weekends, and the money I got from them was enough to get me breakfast at school, while lunch was provided for free. Jan also taught me about food stamps and even took me to the city to apply for them. And when school and food stamps and hunting weren't enough, I found other ways to keep my belly full.

There were two main grocery stores in Fairbanks, Market Basket and Foodland. I learned pretty quickly that when food went past its expiry date, it had to be thrown out. Most of it was too rotten for even a hungry kid to eat, but some of it was perfectly good, and the people who worked at the stores never shooed me away when they found me rooting through their dumpsters.

Charlie came back in early 1976. He'd been working Upslope for a long time, but one day after school, I noticed a truck on his property and saw someone walking around near the shell of the cabin. When Charlie glanced toward me as I approached him, he looked as though he'd seen a ghost. "What the absolute living fuck," he mumbled.

I don't know if it was the shock of me being in Alaska, me showing up on his property, or me simply being alive. Truth is, I never had much of a relationship with Charlie at all, but he was still family. To Charlie's credit, he would do his part in the months to come and help me as much as his circumstances and our history allowed.

As we chatted, I learned that he'd not only been working up in the oil fields on the North Slope but gotten married along the way to a woman named Ellen. Their rough plan was to finish the cabin and eventually move in. Later I led Charlie down the road and showed him my wall tent. "Nice work, little sister," he said as he nodded his head approvingly.

I saw Charlie fairly regularly after that, though mostly as I walked past his building site after school on my way to the tent. Our interactions were friendly but brief, and I got the feeling that although he was happy to see me for a few minutes, that was about all the time he wanted to spend with me. I understood. We were family but strangers all the same.

One day, Charlie surprised me by asking if I wanted to help him with the cabin. I'd never done construction work but took to it immediately. The sense of satisfaction I got from being able to step back at the end of a day and look at what I'd built was infectious, though it came to an abrupt end when I came face-to-face with Charlie's temper one evening. I accidentally stepped on a loose PVC pipe and broke it, after which Charlie launched into a flurry of wrath and expletives that brought me right back to Illinois. I shrank away in fear and in that moment realized being that close was too much for either one of us.

So I continued to do my own thing, which primarily amounted to school and work. I was keenly motivated to graduate as soon as possible so I could either go on to college or get on with my working life. Luckily, fate interceded when I learned about the ultimate Alaskan loophole: I didn't actually need to *attend* classes at North Pole High to pass them. As long as I demonstrated "mastery of the curriculum"—which turned out to be a grade of 65 or better on the year-end exam—I would pass. Age was not a factor. It didn't matter if you were six, eleven, seventeen, or seventy-five… anybody could do it.

Once I found out such an option existed, I took it in my teeth and ran: Graduating became my sole purpose. By the time the school year ended in 1976, I was not quite thirteen years old and had just finished tenth grade.

There were other reasons why I wanted to be done with school, most of them social. I enjoyed living on my own in the tent, but my housing and family situations precluded me from having any sort of good friends: Hanging out at my place after school was definitely *not* an option. Not that anyone really wanted to, anyway. Adolescent girls can be cruel under the best of circumstances, and I was walking around in lost-and-found castoffs and army-dump hand-me-downs. Also, without the benefit of running water, hygiene was not a big thing for me. I regularly found myself the butt of their jokes.

I'd learned to gird myself against the barbs of my peers, though, and turned to the outdoors for peace, joy, and acceptance, just like I'd done for as long as I could remember. In the darkness of winter, I walked the lonely trails around my tent as the snow cascaded softly around me, whispering through the trees like a million untold spirits. When the skies were clear, I lay on my back and watched the northern lights dance overhead in an ever-changing blossom of reds, greens, and purples that continued for hours at a time. And just as I'd done in my cabin, I went to sleep on most nights listening to the far-off cries of a distant pack of wolves as they traveled the mountain passes in search of prey.

I'd continue to pass year-end exams until I graduated North Pole High in 1977, a couple of weeks before I turned fourteen. But before I did, the school graced me with one other gift, one I wouldn't have gotten anywhere else: a private pilot's license. As part of the school curriculum, students could choose either driver's education or ground school, which was a no-brainer for me. I wouldn't be able to get my official pilot's license until I turned sixteen, but there was nothing that said I had to be a minimum age to participate in ground school. So I took it…along with all the other twelfth graders.

The summer of 1977 arrived, and the world lay before me like a blank slate. I had just turned fourteen but had proven to myself that I could make it on my own. And now with school done, I was free to choose my own future. But nothing was going to happen without money, so I decided I needed more of an income than the Powalskis could provide. I started out by landing a construction job at Chena Hot Springs, where nobody ever asked how old I was. Maybe I looked older than fourteen, but it's more likely that they didn't care.

When summer ended, I retreated to my wall tent and found work in Fairbanks, hitching rides to town with other people living on the Chena road who worked in the city. I landed a variety of part-time jobs, all of which I pieced together to make more money than I knew what to do with. It was a wild time in Alaska; as a waitress at the legendary Tick Tock Drive-In—where I wore roller skates and delivered trays of burgers, fries, milkshakes, and soda pop to carloads of customers—pipeline workers back in town from the North Slope regularly tipped me in $100 bills. The tips were even better at the Red Dog Saloon, where I worked as a cocktail waitress, though the clientele was much "handsier." Nobody ever asked how old I was, so I never bothered telling. In a place where lawlessness was a matter of state pride, big boobs were enough to get me hired, even at fourteen.

In time, my savings grew, and when spring rolled around, I had a tidy little sum. I wasn't motivated by money, but at the same time I recognized that if I wanted to do something with my life beyond serving beer to drunken pipeline workers, I'd need some.

Charlie and Ellen finished their cabin that spring and asked me to come for dinner one Saturday after I'd finished at the Red Dog. When I walked in, though, my life flipped upside down: Standing in the living room was my mother.

My mother.

I'll never know if the whole thing was set up beforehand or if it was just some ironic twist of fate that brought us there at the same time. In the end, though, it didn't matter. Mom waltzed toward me like she'd never left.

"Susan!" she exclaimed. "I'm back! You're looking well. Have you lost weight?" I was struck dumb, too shocked to say a word. My mother didn't seem to notice. "And this," she said, indicating a man sitting on Charlie's couch, "is Richard. He's going to be your new dad!"

Time stopped. I was frozen, my arms hanging lifeless at my side and mouth agape. I felt as if I'd left my body and was witnessing a fictional scene from above. Then I began to tremble as tears welled up in my eyes. I was a child again and wanted to run into my mother's arms and have her hug me until the pain went away. But two years on my own had taught me I didn't need her to live a successful, happy life. I was strong. I was independent. And I was on my own.

I took a deep breath and squeezed my eyes hard to stop the tears from coming. If I had been capable of feeling complex emotions, I may have simply exploded. Was it rage? Relief? Sadness? Disbelief?

Likely a combination of all four, but I couldn't identify them, so I didn't know. So instead of screaming or crying or running out the door, I simply spoke. "He is *not* my fucking dad," I growled.

"Don't you swear at me," she said, giving me a stern look, a look that seemed to convey her belief that somehow she still had a say in my choice of words.

I was as tall as her now, so I squared my shoulders and looked directly at her with a glare that could freeze lava. "*Do not* tell me what to do," I hissed slowly and clearly. "I have no idea where you've been, who you've been with, or even if you were alive. So don't think for a second that you can walk into my life and tell me what to do…including who is or isn't going to be my dad."

She clamped her mouth shut, her smile fading to a thin line. I was angry and confused, and more than anything I wanted to be alone in my wall tent. But as I watched her face fall, I realized that for all the heartache that our relationship had brought into my life, I didn't hate her. In fact, there was a part of me that was actually glad for my mother. Maybe she had tamed her demons. But if she hadn't, it would not come at my expense.

CHAPTER 3

RETURNS

The days and weeks that followed were a maelstrom of emotional upheaval and change. Without taking a look back at my family members gathered in the living room of Charlie and Ellen's cabin, I stormed to the door, where I grabbed my jacket, shoved my feet into my boots, and left without saying another word to anyone. I needed to process my mother's resurrection on my own time and in my own space. The problem, of course, was that if Charlie hadn't already shown her my living quarters, he would do so very soon. I needed to get away…and I knew just the place. The next morning I packed my backpack and started walking down the Chena road toward my old cabin.

Unlike my previous trips, I didn't hide in the woods but instead hitched the first ride I could get with someone headed out toward the hot springs. I wanted to get there as quickly as possible, if only to luxuriate in the anonymity of the forest around me. I'd visited the cabin from time to time over the previous two years and knew I wouldn't find anyone—or anything—living there.

The elderly man in a battered Ford F-100 who picked me up gave me a sideways glance when I told him to stop on the otherwise nondescript section of road beyond the unmarked trail to the cabin. "Thanks for the lift," I said as I grabbed the backpack and opened the door.

"You sure this is where you wanna get out, honey?" he asked. "The hot springs are just a few miles up the road."

"I'm sure," I replied as I closed the door and gave it a couple of hard pats with the palm of my hand, my signal for him to get going. The man drove off, and I turned onto the narrow trail that led to my refuge. The light was fading and the path still partially covered with the patchwork of snow that characterized spring, but I knew the way like the back of my hand. Once inside, I lit a fire, rolled out my sleeping bag on the floor, and then lay down and cried.

I hadn't afforded myself the opportunity to cry much since the day I first realized my mother wasn't coming back, and the emotions I'd been holding back burst out of me like a torrent. I cried for the family I'd left behind somewhere in Illinois. I cried for the father I'd never known. I cried for the little girl I once was and the childhood I knew I would never get back. Eventually the sobs subsided and I fell asleep.

When I woke up, the fire had gone cold, and I shivered as I pulled my coat around me. It was still dark outside, but I knew it wouldn't be long before the muted glow of sunrise would wash across the land, a symphony of pale pinks, purples, and oranges reflecting off the snow outside the cabin. I pulled on my boots, walked outside, and simply stood there with my arms held out wide as I turned slow circles in space as I looked up at the lightening sky above me. In the grand panoply of my teenage life, I had only called the cabin home for a handful of weeks, but during that time something had changed inside me. I had come to appreciate the fact that I could survive on my own, no matter how harsh the circumstances around me. As I stood there twirling slowly between the cabin and the river, those feelings came rushing back. Yes, my mother had returned. And yes, she was with yet another man. But I'd survived much worse, and I'd survive this.

By the time I returned to my wall tent a few days later, my head was clear. For the first time since my mother and I had pulled up in the Suburban and set up camp on Charlie's property, Alaska felt too small for me. I'd toyed with the idea of going to college ever since I graduated high school, and with my mother back in my life, leaving seemed like the right thing to do. Several months and a few college applications later, though, I came face-to-face with an uncomfortable reality: The rest of the country did not operate in the same wild and woolly way that Alaska did. There were rules, and people seemed content to abide by them. They didn't accept my high school diploma (apparently Koyukon didn't meet the foreign-language requirement), and I didn't get into college.

Meanwhile, my mother and her new hubby Richard stayed out of my way, an arrangement that suited me perfectly. I had done fine on my own since my mother's disappearance and didn't need any help. To the outside world, mine was a life categorically *not* suited for a teenage girl. To me, though, I lacked nothing. I had food and shelter and a little bit of money, and the wild world around me fulfilled me in a way that humans never had. Plus, *I* was the only one responsible for my well-being. I didn't need to ask anyone's permission; I did what I wanted…when and where and how I wanted. I reveled in that fact, wore it like a suit of armor. I was Sir Fucking Lancelot of Alaska.

Then, one evening in late spring as I was pondering the possibility of making a career at the Red Dog Saloon, Richard showed up at my tent. "Charlie tells me that you are having problems with your college applications."

I was curious to see him there but even more curious about what he was saying. "I am," I said, slightly puzzled. "Why?"

He looked down at the ground and sighed. "OK, here's the deal. I'm taking a job as an oil engineer in Saudi Arabia with a company called Aramco, but they might not hire me if they know I've got a teenage stepdaughter living on her own in the Alaskan woods."

"What do they care?" I asked.

"The company used to be American but is now mostly owned by the Saudis," he explained. "As part of that, foreign employees are expected to respect Saudi customs. And having a child who lives by herself in a tent definitely doesn't align with Saudi customs. Like I said, it's probably not a big deal, but they perform extensive background checks on all new employees. I can't take the chance."

"I see your conundrum."

"But I think I have a solution," Richard said as he sat down in a wooden chair. "What if I get you into boarding school down south? You can get a legitimate high school degree and then go to college from there." In the end, I knew he was only looking out for himself, but if I could ride his palpable discomfort into boarding school and college, why not? That September I left Alaska for Steamboat Springs, Colorado, where I was enrolled in twelfth grade at a place called the Lowell Whiteman School, all bought and paid for by the newest man in my mother's life.

As much as my mother tried to make small talk on the drive to the Fairbanks airport, I said little in return. Instead I merely looked out the window as the magical forests I had called home for the previous three years sped by in a blur of greens and grays. *How funny a thing life is*, I thought.

As a private prep school serving some of the country's most elite families, Lowell Whiteman was a universe away from my wall tent. I was the squarest peg that anyone had ever attempted to shove in that round hole of privilege and wealth, but I put my head down, ignored the occasional jibes and sideways glances of my classmates, and aced all my subjects. In my free time, I worked as a babysitter, got into an ill-advised relationship with an older man, and found respite in the Rocky Mountains of the American West. But as the school year wound to a close, I found myself longing for the place I had left behind. Suddenly, college wasn't as important to me as I once thought. My heart had been damaged by a man I never should have gotten involved with, and I needed to heal. Alaska was calling me home.

Charlie had left Fairbanks for New England, where he was attending guitar-building school, so I moved in with Ellen in their cabin on the Chena road and picked up my life where I had left off ten months before. Construction of the Alaska Pipeline had finished in the year I was gone, but the insane amounts of money that were thrown around before I left remained, and the destruction that money left in its wake was evident. Drugs and booze were everywhere, and Alaska only increased in its lawlessness and dysfunction. I dabbled in the softer side of the drug spectrum, smoking weed with Ellen once in a while, but never crossed over to the coke and heroin that other people used. If anything, the previous few years had taught me that maintaining control was essential to survival.

Instead, I focused on the two things I did best: working and exploring. And when I needed time to myself, I disappeared to my tent or the cabin, both of which had been largely untouched since I left the previous summer, except for the shrews that had decided to move into the tent. I was content in my life and felt more rooted to the place with each passing day. And yet I couldn't shake the feeling that the relationship I'd left behind in Colorado was meant for something more. So on the day I turned eighteen, I decided to go back and give it another try.

It didn't take me long to realize what an ill-advised decision it was. Through the lens of time, I look back on that brief period and realize I knew absolutely nothing about how to handle myself in a romantic situation or what to look for in a partner. I'd had no experiences with boys through school, no high school crushes to serve as my testing ground for the complexity and nuances of romantic adult relationships. All I knew is that someone was *interested* in me, told me I was loved. A few months after I returned to Steamboat Springs, I left again. This time, though, my path home didn't go directly north. Not at first, anyway.

From Colorado I moved to Mexico, which seemed as far away from the relationship as I could get. He followed, proclaiming eternal dedication, but it was over. I got a job, got my heart broken again, learned to windsurf. It was a wild, tempestuous time full of sun and surf and old Mexican women rolling flour tortillas by hand in the hidden alleys of Cozumel. And then, like a specter from beyond that refused to loosen its grip on my soul, my mother found me again.

How she managed to track me down, I'll never know because I never asked and she never told me. But when my boyfriend's sister handed me the phone and my mother told me she was dying of cancer, I knew my days of tropical idyll were about to come to a screeching halt. Days later I packed up my Mexican life and began the long journey to Vancouver, Washington, where I learned my now-single mother was *not* dying of cancer. In fact, she didn't have cancer at all.

Why did I go? It's a question I've asked myself for decades. This was the woman who had put me to sleep by telling me how awful I was. This was the woman who had taken me away from my home in Illinois and dragged me to Alaska, only to leave me to die. This was the woman who reappeared in my life only to ship me off again for the sake of her own interests. If ever there was anyone who clearly did *not* deserve the grace of my assistance, it was her. But I went anyway.

In the end, I think the decision was twofold. For one, she was my *mother*, and as woeful as she was in that role, she was the only one I had or would ever have. And that, in and of itself, meant an awful lot to me. My biological father was a mystery, Jack and Joe and Richard all just wisps of memory. So I only had one parent, and my sense of obligation to her was incredibly strong. On the other hand, I also think I had a deep-rooted need to try to please her, to gain her approval and affirmation. She never told me I was good or worthy, and somehow I needed to prove that to her. And for the next few weeks, I tried my damnedest to make that happen.

When she wasn't working, we went on walks along the Columbia River, crossed the water, and went shopping in neighboring Portland from time to time. I cooked her meals, even brushed her hair. But through it all, the undercurrent of discontent that had always formed the foundation of our relationship remained. Gone were the days of her telling me how to live my life, but in some ways it was painfully evident that she didn't like me very much. I worked hard for her approval, perhaps even a fleeting sign of affection, but none came. Eventually the feelings between us grew thin and stretched, like a piece of dough that's been pulled apart too far, only to snap and flop down lifelessly. So shortly before my nineteenth birthday, I took the few dollars I had left to my name and returned to Fairbanks.

Once there, I picked up where I left off, though this time I got an apartment in the city itself, which only made it easier to work. Eighty-hour work weeks became the norm, and even though I was paying rent for the first time in my life, my bank account grew with each paycheck. Among my several jobs was a cocktail waitress gig at a joint called Tommy's Elbow Room, a rowdy, reckless sort of place that epitomized the city's bar scene of the '80s.

For a year and a half, my life became incredibly predictable. I worked almost constantly but took every free moment to hunt, fish, and explore. On the banks of the Tanana River, I took down my first moose, a massive, majestic bull that provided more meat than I could ever hope to consume. As I crouched over the animal and felt the last traces of its life sip away, I realized what a privilege—and responsibility—it was to hold that kind of power in my hands.

"Thank you," I whispered to the moose, slowly stroking its massive neck. "Your death has not been in vain." After, I sat for a long time on the bank of the river, my arms wrapped around my knees as the late-summer sun lowered in the sky behind me. In that place, I was at peace. I knew that no matter what the world threw at me, all I needed to do was retreat to the elemental serenity that defined the wilderness and all would be well. And then everything changed.

Randy Payne walked into my life on a cold December night in 1983. A young, fit soldier stationed at Fort Wainwright, Randy had a killer smile and a personality to match. When he spoke to me for the first time with a Southern drawl too damn delightful to ignore, I was smitten. It was a feeling I hadn't allowed myself to acknowledge for a while, but when I finally gave myself permission to open up to that young soldier, I went head over heels.

The Randy Payne chapter of my life was as eventful as it was short-lived. A few months after we met, we were married. After the honeymoon phase wore off, we settled into a comfortable rhythm.

I'm not sure we achieved marital bliss, but we got along well and shared more good moments than bad ones. By the time I was twenty-one, I was pregnant with my first child. Then Randy was reassigned to Fort Campbell, Kentucky. I loved Alaska with every fiber of my being, but I'd tied the knot and was carrying Randy's baby. Plus, nobody marries a military man without realizing that moving is likely going to be part of her future.

In time, I wrapped my head around the idea, even got excited by it. But even as we drove away and began the four-thousand-mile journey to the other corner of the country, I knew that somehow, some way, I'd be back. What I didn't realize was that I'd be doing it as a widow.

Randy died of a brain tumor shortly after we got to Kentucky, an experience that was as surreal as it was heart-wrenching. I'd just turned twenty-one and was eight months pregnant, and we'd sold the car a few days after we arrived. With little other choice, I got on a bus headed northwest. I had convinced myself that living in Kentucky for a few years would actually be fun, but with Randy gone that notion evaporated like the morning mist over the Chena River. I wanted to go home.

Three days later I'd made it as far as my mother's place, where she was still living in Vancouver, Washington. A few weeks later, on Veterans Day, 1984, Jennifer Payne was born.

Life as a new mother is challenging under the best of circumstances. Throw in the fact that my husband was dead, I had terrible parental role models as a kid, and I was living with my mother and, well…you can imagine just how difficult it was. Nevertheless, I was determined to not bring up my child the same way I had been raised. I would love her and respect her and always be open to hear whatever she had to say. Good or bad or ugly, I'd be ready for it all. Then, before baby Jennie was even a year old, lightning struck when I was working at a Portland bar and bumped into Eddie Aikens.

He was one of the most beautiful men I'd ever seen, lean and fit like a wolf, with dark eyes that penetrated my soul the first time he looked at me. But the one physical attribute that will forever define Eddie is his dark, waist-length ringlets. It is without a doubt the most beautiful hair I've ever seen in my life. I may have only possessed the emotional capacity of a Ritz cracker, but I knew enough to know that I loved Eddie the moment I met him. Days later—*days*—Jennie and I moved in with him. On June 13, 1986, we were married.

The wedding was as far from traditional as Portland was from Fairbanks. Eddie was a haircutter by trade, but his clients were strictly limited to the various biker clubs that called the area home. So rather than use a local church for our nuptials, Eddie and I instead rented a park, one large enough to accommodate the various members of the Gypsy Jokers, Hells Angels, Brother

Speed, and Christ's Disciples who wanted to see "Haircutter Ed" tie the knot.

Biker etiquette dictates that no violence take place when rival clubs attend a common event, but when our guests showed up with what looked like dozens of cases of Jack Daniel's in tow, Ed and I were worried that something might happen anyway. Rather than stick around to watch it blow up in front of us, we asked his mom to watch Jennie for a couple of days and then took off on his Harley for Reno. The next day we were married in a civil service at The Hitching Post wedding chapel and I became Susan Aikens. Nine months later, our son Jesse was born.

In the years that followed, our family settled into a routine that most other people would likely have defined as "comfortable." Ed was never particularly motivated by money, and his sporadic, part-time work schedule did little to feather our financial nest. So I did what I did best and picked up several jobs, from construction to cocktail waitressing, while he looked after the kids. In whatever spare time we had, we whiled away the hours in the lush green forests of the Pacific Northwest. And on those rare occasions when I actually had an entire weekend off, we'd pile in the car and drive east to Mount Hood National Forest, where we'd spend a couple of blissful days away from the conventional and all-too-orderly life that suburban Portland afforded.

It was in those moments that I felt more myself than I had since I first left Fairbanks with Randy several years before. I'd wake up while Eddie and the kids still slept soundly in the tent, being careful to unzip the door as quietly as possible as I stole outside to feel the day dawn around me. Then I'd wander down some lonely trail to the middle of the forest where, surrounded by groves of hemlock and cedar trees, I'd sit and simply *be.* Around me the forest would slowly come to life, and I'd feel my soul ignited anew as the jackhammer *thunk thunk thunk* of a woodpecker's beak echoed through the misty hills. One time, I watched in awe as a mama black bear and her two cubs trundled by on the far side of Lost Lake, never noticing me as I sat, cross-legged and stock-still, on a stump in the woods on the other side. I loved being a mother and a wife, but I rarely felt more alive than I did then.

Meanwhile, our life in Portland proceeded with a predictability and structure I found suffocating. Everybody—especially Eddie's siblings, who also lived in the city—expected me to be a "perfect" suburban wife, barefoot and pregnant and giddily seated in the first pew at church on Sundays...but that wasn't the life I had signed up for.

So I worked; sometimes Eddie did too. The kids started to grow up, and I watched in awe as their problems and questions slowly evolved from tiny things like tying their shoelaces and *choo-chooing* the food into their little mouths to friends and romances and grades and drinking and fights. I loved my family but at the same time felt like something inside me was slowly shriveling up. My soul, maybe? I was so busy trying to keep our family afloat and manage the day-to-day challenges of being a parent and a wife that I didn't always notice it. But when we got away for those weekends and I snuck out to be on my own while Eddie and the kids slept, I knew the light inside me was slowly fading.

Eddie saw it too and to his credit said was willing to try life in Alaska to help me get back to being me. We visited various parts of the state: Fairbanks, Juneau, Sitka, Haines. But none of them fit, and we always ended up being pulled back to the Portland area, where Eddie's parents lived. Eddie liked to joke that he was more John Wayne and I was more Grizzly Adams, but there was more truth in it than either one of us knew. The million-dollar question, though, was whether the two could live together in harmony.

My body answered that question before my mind did. I was exhausted, working six and sometimes seven days a week at a variety of jobs so we could try to buy a house, in addition to helping Eddie's parents stay on top of his mother Loretta's medical bills. Together it all added up to an incredible amount of stress for me, and I started to short-circuit.

At first, my seizure-like episodes were almost imperceptible and easy to ignore. But as time progressed, they only worsened. One morning, after a particularly long night at the bar, I found myself sprawled out on our bedroom floor, Eddie kneeling over me and looking like he'd seen a ghost.

"Sue… Sue!" he cried. "Jesus… Are you OK?"

I tried to sit up but couldn't. I felt as if I'd just run a marathon, my body physically spent, my heart locked in a box. "What happened?" I asked.

"You collapsed on the floor. But really slow, like you knew what you were doing. It was awful. You started jerking, like you were having a seizure or something, your head rolling from side to side. It would stop for a moment and then start up again. Then, just when I thought it was over, you started doing it again, only this time you were screaming, 'No, no, no!'"

I pushed myself up on my elbows and looked at Ed. He was confused and scared. I knew it was a sign, though. Something had to give.

But it didn't…not at first, anyway. The seizures continued, and eventually I was diagnosed with something called psychogenic nonepileptic episodes, seizure-like incidents that differ from traditional seizures in that they're caused by psychological factors like stress rather than abnormal electrical activity in the brain. Eventually I was put on medication, and when that didn't work, they took my driver's license away. Suddenly life became a whole lot more stressful.

Fate intervened a couple of months later when I received a letter from a friend of mine who lived in Fairbanks, a family doctor I'd also gotten to know socially. Dr. Metcalf and I had actually grown quite close in the years after I returned from Colorado, and we met for coffee every month or so. So when his letter arrived, I was very pleasantly surprised to learn he was coming through Portland and wanted to get together for lunch.

"Wow," he said after we hugged and sat down across the table from one another. "You seem...different. I thought you were happy down here." I immediately burst out crying and then proceeded to dump all my problems on him. He listened intently as he sipped his coffee, not saying a word. When I finished, he finally spoke.

"Sue," he said, "look around you. This is *nice*, but it isn't *you*. You don't belong in this world." I knew he was right and simply sat there nodding. "Here's what I suggest you do. I'm actually on my way to Brownsville, Texas, where I'm going to be working for a while. I think you should get down there too. Texas isn't Alaska, but there are lots of things to do outside, and at least you'll be away from the pressure of Eddie's family. Plus," he added, "you need to be off these drugs you're taking. You're not an epileptic."

Less than a month later, Jesse, Jennie, and I rolled up to a house I'd rented in Harlingen, Texas...minus Eddie, who felt too tied to his parents to leave them. A month later he moved in too after he realized that being apart was too difficult.

Texas was a whole new world. My workdays were long, and we didn't know a soul, but I felt freer there than I had in years. Lighter. Wide-open spaces. Not too many people. Slack rules. Things began to click again, and as promised, Dr. Metcalf slowly weaned me off the meds. Sometimes the four of us drove the forty-odd miles over the border and took the kids to Mexico. On other evenings we walked around downtown Harlingen, holding hands, eating shaved ice and soft-serve ice cream. And when it got dark, we ran around our backyard catching lightning bugs and putting them in mason jars. But when Eddie's father Jim suffered a heart attack, our Texas experiment came to an abrupt end.

"We gotta go back, Sue," he said after he got off the phone with his mother. "They need us." I agreed: Loretta and Jim were my family too, and there was no way we were going to turn our backs on them in their time of need. So the Aikens train rolled out of Texas and made its way back to the Pacific Northwest, first Portland, followed by stints in Washougal and Port Townsend, Washington, where we were still close enough to help look after Eddie's parents but far enough away to feel *away*. The seizures didn't return, but I knew it was only a matter of time before the confines of society outside Alaska began to wear me down again.

Eddie's father Jim passed away in 1999, which was as gut-wrenching for me as it was eye-opening. I loved that man; he was perhaps the first father figure I'd ever had who treated me with genuine kindness and respect. At the same time, though, Jim's death opened my eyes to the fact that life is a short and precious gift…one I felt like I was giving away with each day that went by with me trapped in the bubble of my life. Then, when Loretta developed a heart condition and subsequently underwent open-heart surgery, I knew what Eddie was going to say even before he sat beside me on the couch one evening: He wanted to go home. The problem was, so did I.

It was our Alamo, our moment of reckoning. Two people strongly connected and committed to one another but with hearts pulling them in different directions. Eddie was a generous, considerate son, one who would always be there for his mother, especially after her husband was no longer there to care for her. I loved Eddie and my children and Loretta like I'd never loved anyone before. But each day that passed after we returned to Portland was a heavier burden on my spirit. My children were now in their mid-teens and happily ensconced in their own lives...ones I was a smaller part of every month. I didn't begrudge them that reality; I saw it as a normal rite of passage. But no longer was my love and sense of responsibility enough to keep my head above water in the rising tide of discontent. Deep down I knew that as much as I loved Jesse and Jennie, I couldn't be the role model I needed to be for them while at the same time living with a tortured soul.

With each passing day, the draw to return north grew stronger. I dreamed of the northern lights, the untamed places, a society unbound by rules. I longed to trek through the bush with a rifle on my shoulder, the rush of an icy creek the only sound filling my ears. I needed to feel the snow on my face again. But each time I thought of returning, the gravity of my family and my responsibilities in the Lower World pulled me back down. Every day, duty and authenticity battled for dominance inside me.

The tug of war on my heart continued for weeks, until Eddie and I went camping again. I arose early, as I often did, and stole away into the forest to be alone with nature. Slowly the sun rose from the east as always, poking its way through breaks in the trees and shining ethereal rays of light on dewy patches of earth below. Suddenly a breeze picked up, and the smells of the forest washed across my face. As they did, one of them hit me like a freight train. It was subtle but unmistakable all the same: high-bush cranberries. For a moment, I was back in Alaska, a young girl picking berries in a field by an abandoned cabin she'd come to call home.

It was the sign I'd been looking for all along, a gut punch that made me realize that as much as I'd been trying, I would *never* blossom as part of the Lower World. Whether I wanted to admit it or not, there was an undeniable touchstone inside me that *was* Alaska. I inhaled deeply and took in the smell for a few seconds, felt the hope rush through my veins. And I knew.

I needed to go find me again.

CHAPTER 4

THE TRAPPER

The fire had burned down to embers in the long Alaskan night, and it was freezing inside the cabin as the darkness outside slowly grew to a furtive dawn, not much more at that time of year than gentle streaks of purple haze stretching lazily across the winter sky. Alaska is one of the few places on Earth where overnight frost regularly forms on the *inside* of windows, but that's what you get when indoor heat sources can't keep up with minus-fifty-degree temperatures outside. Plus, the little log cabin was likely close to a hundred years old and not particularly well insulated. Despite my best efforts, the chinking—the moss and lichen I used to seal the horizontal gaps between the logs—hadn't done much to keep out the night chill. I pulled off the caribou and wolf hides that covered my sleeping bag, crawled out, and stoked the fire inside the wood stove. Then I placed my blackened coffeepot on top, rubbed my eyes, and shoved my feet—still clad in two pairs of gray wool socks with red stripes around the calves—into my felt-lined winter boots. It was time to feed the team of eight Alaskan malamutes staked outside the cabin.

I hadn't arrived at the cabin by accident. After that moment of realization when I *smelled* Alaska and felt the irrepressible desire to return home, I knew it made no sense to deny my destiny any longer. I had tried my damnedest to be a good mother and wife and find peace in the Lower 48—even sacrificed a good part of my soul along the way—but I was dying inside. With time, that cancer of discontent would have spread throughout my body and, one way or another, eventually killed me. Eddie saw it too. I was no longer the wild child he had fallen in love with. Years of structure and conformity, coupled with the expectations and disapproval of his extended family, had sucked the life out of me. Ed had once said that when I walked into a room the entire place filled up with the light I emitted. Fifteen years later, that light had been extinguished. I'd gotten good at going through the motions of our daily existence—even managed to find joy in the occasional moment—but I was a shadow of my true self.

There were a million reasons to stay and try to make it work, and I knew every one of them. But I was failing, and Eddie knew it as well as I did. One evening after I finished a shift on the construction site and the kids were out with their friends, I sat him down on the couch, poured us a couple glasses of whiskey, and told him what he knew had been coming for a long time.

"I'm sorry, Ed," I said as I took a long draw on the glass and fire spread through my insides. "I can't do it anymore. I don't like who I'm turning into, and I'm sure that pretty soon you won't like me, either. In the end, this world is not for me. I'm so sorry." Tears welled up in Eddie's eyes as he gripped his glass tightly with both hands, tucked his elbows into the crease where his thighs met his midsection, and leaned in toward me, rocking gently back and forth with sadness and fear. It was like finally saying goodbye to someone who dies after a long battle with an illness: You know it's coming, but when it happens, it still hurts like hell.

He grabbed my neck and kissed me hard before pulling away. "Know one thing," he said, his dark-brown eyes locked onto mine like the first time we met. "I love you. It hasn't always been perfect, but I've never stopped loving you."

"I know," I said.

The weeks that followed were a blur of activity as I planned to return to the only place I've ever felt truly at peace. Of course the first order of business was to sit down with the kids and explain what was happening. Their lives were going to look very different in the months and years to come, and I wanted to make sure they had the chance to share all their feelings about it with me, the good, the bad, and the ugly. That said, my revelation didn't come as much of a surprise to either one of them, either; apparently they'd been preparing themselves for that eventuality for a while. We may not give teenagers credit for much these days, but Jennie and Jesse knew me better than I realized.

In the quiet moments between the conversations and activity that my decision had spurred, I wrestled with a rainbow of conflicting emotions that seemed to rise out of nowhere and color my insides for a couple of hours. Guilt and relief, sadness and elation, mourning and celebration… They all took turns dwelling within me, and I welcomed each one into the crowded living room of my heart, to the extent that I could even understand them. Yet as much as I was able to quell those emotions by focusing on the nitty-gritty of what needed to get done before my departure, there was one question that echoed through my brain and refused to grow quiet: *Was I turning into my mom?*

She had abandoned me when I was just entering my teens, and here I was leaving the three most important people in my life so I could follow my own path more than two thousand miles away. Such disturbing similarities aside, I knew this situation was radically different than the one I had lived through as a child. There would be no surprises, no squelched emotions for the sake of self-preservation. I discussed my decision at length with the kids, and Eddie was nothing but supportive. But still, you don't have a childhood like mine and not feel the skeletons of your past peeking at you from inside the closet.

In the end, the four of us decided that we would keep in touch as best we could, but in an era where the internet was still a fledgling technology (and Alaska was decades behind the rest of the country), we knew our communications would be sporadic at best. That said, when we drove to the airport together for my flight to Fairbanks, the mood was anything but somber. Somehow we all knew this was the right thing. I had raised confident, self-sufficient, and intelligent kids who needed me less and less every day. Jennie was just about finished with high school and would soon be leaving our nest; Jesse was a couple of years younger but had already been in a relationship with the same girl for a few years and was much more interested in spending time with Megan than he was with me. As for Eddie and me, we would stay married and see if we could make the long-distance thing work.

A few hours later, the plane circled low over Fairbanks, and I gazed out the window in anticipation of what lay ahead. Below me, the late-afternoon sun reflected off the Chena River as it carved gentle curves in the land, snaking its way toward the southern edge of the White Mountains on the horizon. On either side, the dense, untamed boreal forest waited, its secrets unknown to all except those who ventured within. Moments later we touched down, and for the first time in what seemed like forever, I felt the blood pumping through my veins. I cried a little and kissed my family goodbye in my mind. Then I walked out of the airport, got my first good whiff of clean Alaskan air, and smiled.

Like the rivers, everything changes course eventually.

Of course Fairbanks was the place I'd chosen to begin my resurrection. Anchorage (which many Alaskans referred to as *California* back then) had never been attractive to me—too big, too ordered, too much like the life I was trying to escape—and everything I had known and loved about Alaska began with the area around Fairbanks. But even as I threw my bag down on my friend Laura's couch, I knew I would only be crashing in her apartment long enough to figure out my next steps. It would have been easy to nail down a job or two and fall back into my old habits, but I hadn't left my family behind just to rejoin the rat race in another city. My heart was calling me further afield, to the wild, untrammeled places I'd never seen before.

That's not to say I didn't work upon my return because I did... but only enough to save the money I needed to fund the next stage of my life. I had no idea what that would look like, but I wasn't bothered by such details. I had faith that the universe would present me with the right opportunity when it was ready to do so; all I had to do was stay open to it. Months later, it did.

Alaska is the largest state in the Union (and more than twice the size of Texas, the second-largest state), some 663,000 square miles of rugged terrain and abundant natural resources that have beguiled the hearts and minds of poets and adventurers alike since it was first acquired from Russia on March 30, 1867, by Secretary of State William H. Seward for $7.2 million, or about 2 cents an acre. It boasts a mind-boggling array of topography and landscapes, everything from mountains (including Denali, the tallest peak in North America at 20,310 feet) to rainforests to endless tracts of windswept tundra. It experiences the wildest temperature swings in the United States and has more coastline than every other state combined.

Yet for all its vastness, that same Alaska—at least the Alaska I know—is an incredibly small place when it comes to people. Word of mouth travels quickly, reputation is everything, and the friends you make at one point in your life invariably reappear again at some other place and time to play a role in your story. People care about each other, will go out of their way to help one another in times of need, and never forget a good deed. So it didn't take long for Fairbanks to realize I had returned. Suddenly my social life was electric, and I spent as much of my downtime wandering the hillsides as I did in the coffee shops and bars, chatting with anyone and everyone who wanted to catch up on the circumstances of my life.

With those conversations, an idea began to coalesce in my mind. Dogs and dog teams were as Alaskan as the snow itself, an integral part of the state's history, culture, and even survival. First Nations people used them for transporting people and goods over vast distances before White men ever set foot in the state. Dogs were indispensable during the gold rush era of the late nineteenth and early twentieth centuries and hauled supplies, mail, and heavy equipment over snowy trails that horses and wagons couldn't hope to navigate. Dog mushing was even considered sport in Alaska, where the Iditarod and Yukon Quest—both thousand-mile races that originate in the state—have become the two most famous races of their kind. The more I talked about it, the more I thought about it, and the more I sat with it, I knew this was the opportunity I'd been waiting for.

I'd never owned dogs as a kid (my unique life circumstances prevented me from enjoying such luxuries), but they were never far from my consciousness; everybody had them. More than a few kids attending North Pole High were dogsledded back and forth by their parents and their team; some of the world's most well-known mushers—including George Attla Jr., Lance Mackey, and Susan Butcher—lived and trained in the area. But unlike their lapdog counterparts in the Lower World, dogs in Alaska were more partners in a way of life than they were pets. And that, I realized, was exactly what I wanted.

Owning and running sled dogs would offer the simplicity of animal companionship, to be sure, but also an entry into a way of life that aligned with everything I felt I needed at that point in my own personal narrative. If anything, it would help connect me even more deeply to the land and the rhythms of nature. It would require intense physical effort, but along with that effort came a sense of purpose and a connection with Alaskan traditions that I'd never had before. I thought long and hard about what I'd be getting into, but in the end, the decision was easy. Sled dogs were more than just animals, they were companions in life's journey, the ultimate connection to an existence shaped by purpose and challenge. I was in.

I bought an old truck with the money I'd saved and then slowly built my team. It wasn't as difficult as it sounds. Serious mushers and sledders are constantly turning over their teams for a number of reasons, and dogs regularly become available to anyone who has their ear to the ground. But I had learned too much to take just *any* dog and had zero interest in pansy-ass breeds that I'd need to dig out of the snow every five minutes or that required booties strapped onto their paws. So I began to build a team of freighter dogs, legendary Alaskan sled dogs bred for working rather than racing. Usually giant Alaskan malamutes, freighter dogs could plow their way through conditions and terrain that would stop other animals dead in their tracks. You wouldn't win a race with a freighter dog, but in a war of attrition, they'd be the last soldiers standing.

The next thing on my to-do list was to pick a place I wanted to call home. I'd spent almost all of my Alaska time in and around Fairbanks, and as much as I loved the area, I wanted to see more. I eventually decided to set up my home base in the tiny twin communities of Coldfoot and Wiseman, about 250 miles north of Fairbanks (and above the Arctic Circle) up a lonely gravel road locals called the Haul Road, though its official name was the Dalton Highway.

It wasn't so much that I chose Coldfoot/Wiseman as it fit the bill of what I was looking for. There are not that many communities around Fairbanks to begin with (less than fifteen within a hundred-mile radius), let alone ones that can be reached by a woman in a truck full of dogs and gear. I knew I wanted to go farther north, and Coldfoot/Wiseman was definitely that. Plus, my buddy Clutch (a long-haul trucker) owned a few cabins with land in Wiseman that he rented for cheap, and it would make a perfect home base for my team and me. The area around there, nestled in the arms of the Koyukuk River valley, was reputed to have some of the most beautiful scenery in the state, where the foothills melted slowly to the snowcapped reaches of the mythical Brooks Range beyond. Best of all, both towns played important roles in Alaskan history, particularly during the gold rush era of the late 1800s and early 1900s, and I was keen to learn as much as possible about it. So with winter setting in and the days getting shorter, I loaded my truck and said goodbye to Fairbanks.

The prospect of employment was not lost on me. There were few opportunities in two towns with a combined population of around fifty people, but I had no interest in working anything resembling a traditional job anyway. Nevertheless, money was important even in the farthest reaches of the Last Frontier, and the dogs were not going to feed themselves. The answer, I realized, was about as traditional as I could get. I set my sights on being a trapper.

Like my decision to keep dogs, the choice to live as a trapper was not one I made without serious consideration. Trapping is not just a job, it's a commitment. The work environment is largely outdoors, usually in extreme cold and often surrounded by the dark of Alaskan winter, and the physical demands are legion. I would be away from town for extended periods of time, and during those periods would need to be completely self-reliant. In the spring, warming weather patterns and increasing sunlight would thaw the rivers and turn large parts of my terrain into mud baths, making travel unpredictable at best or at worst stopping my dogs and me dead in our tracks. Communication with the outside world would be virtually nonexistent while I was in the bush, and I'd forever be looking over my shoulder for hungry bears or wolves in search of a quick meal. I'd be responsible for taking care of any illnesses and injuries, not the least of which was the possibility of frostbite and hypothermia. I'd need to find or establish a series of cabins along the trapline, each of which would need to be cleaned up, maintained, and kept warm. And every day I'd have to haul water from a nearby source (assuming I could get through the ice to the free flow below) or melt snow for hours to keep the dogs and me hydrated.

Finally there was the whole question of killing animals for their fur. I realize this issue is a political hot potato and one that elicits strong ethical and emotional responses from people, especially those unfamiliar with the lifestyle or environment I grew up in. But the Alaska I knew and loved was a completely separate world from the rest of the country, and our collective mindset on the relationship between predator and prey is vastly different than most people could ever assume to know. We are hunters and fishers, and killing animals to ensure human survival has been a way of life here for millennia. Of course I didn't *need* to trap to survive, but in the end I made peace with my decision. I would do my best to honor every animal I took, sell the furs I needed to sell, use the hides I needed to keep me warm, and feed the meat to the dogs and me. Believe it or not, the trappers I had come to know were also some of the strongest conservationists I'd ever met, men and women who lived in tune with nature and made compelling arguments that their practices were more sustainable and humane than industrial farming or synthetic material production. Ultimately, I recognized that living a life as a trapper would be one that was as deeply connected to the wilderness as any I had ever known, and I wanted to be a part of it.

My first order of business was establishing a home base in one of Clutch's cabins, a task that required me to furnish it for myself and the eight dogs. I built a doghouse for each one and then lined their wooden floors with hay. Alaskan malamutes are incredibly hearty and can curl up in a ball and sleep quite comfortably in conditions that would kill a human in hours, but at the same time it's nice for them to have a place they can retreat to and rest after a long stint out on the trapline.

The next step was training the team to work together and respect me as their alpha. A male giant Alaskan malamute can weigh as much as two hundred pounds, and they are not animals to be trifled with. I would need to work hard to gain their trust, earn their respect, and turn our group of nine distinct creatures into a single functioning unit. It would require diligence and patience, and over time I would need to understand their behavior and personalities as well as I knew my own. Luckily, I had saved up enough money from the months I lived in Fairbanks to not feel the financial pressure to get back to work right away. So I took my time.

Over the next couple of months, I spent nearly all my waking hours with the dogs, either as a group or individually. With every action I performed, no matter how small, I made sure to assert myself, subtly but clearly, as the alpha of the pack. We would soon be venturing out into extremely challenging conditions, and the only way to ensure our safety was for me to take charge. The dogs could have torn me to bits had they decided to do so, but at the same time they wanted a clear leader to guide them, and that leader was most assuredly me.

So I rewarded them when they did something right and scolded when they stepped out of line. I taught them basic dog commands like *sit* and *stay* and then graduated to sled commands like *hike* (get going), *gee* (turn right), *haw* (turn left), and *whoa* (stop). I dictated their feeding schedule, and eventually we got to the point where the dogs would sit obediently in front of their food and wait for my command before eating. When we traveled together through tight spaces, I always went first, and my body language told them that I was in charge.

Over time, the team and I developed a bond much closer than I initially thought possible. I slowly introduced them to the idea of wearing harnesses and got them used to pulling light loads over short distances. Soon we were making increasingly longer trips along the trails that snaked their way through the spruce forests. The dogs grew accustomed to their position in the pecking order of the team. There were the two lead dogs up front, the ones who bore the responsibility of steering and setting the pace; followed in turn by a pair of swing dogs, which helped guide us through turns; team dogs, the engine in the middle; and finally a pair of wheel dogs, the strongest and sturdiest of the bunch, who handled the bulk of the weight of the sled behind.

In time, we ventured out of the valley and to the west toward the West Fork of the Chandalar River and Chandalar Lake, where I'd eventually lay my trapline. Together the dogs and I learned how to navigate the dizzying array of trails, though my lead dogs seemed to know their way home without much guidance. No matter what the conditions, no matter how deep the snow, no matter how rugged the terrain, those animals pulled the sled like it was the greatest joy they'd ever known. At night we'd return to the cabin, where I'd feed them the high-fat, high-energy diet they needed to keep themselves fueled, usually raw fish and meat mixed with beef tallow, lard, or fish oil, plus warm water they could drink before the Alaskan air froze it solid.

If I'd felt my heart begin to open during my time in Fairbanks, the move to the Koyukuk River valley saw it blossom like a wild rose in spring. With each exhausting sixteen-hour day that passed, I felt closer to myself than I had in years, maybe forever. There were magical moments where the dogs would pull me through a powder blanket of freshly fallen snow, the only sound their breathing and the gentle swish of the sled runners beneath me through an endless sea of white. Sometimes I'd look up to see a caribou pawing at the ground to get at the frozen vegetation beneath or an Arctic fox springing through the air to pounce at whatever unsuspecting rodent was fleeing for its life below. The work was exhausting, the cold numbing, and the land vast. But the joy I felt with each icy breath was as profound as any I'd ever known in my life. I was finally free of the burdens that had weighed on my soul for so long.

Of course, I missed Eddie and the kids, but at the same time, I have never been the type of person to wallow in self-pity or question the choices I've made. Life taught me that dwelling on the sins of the past serves no purpose today, and I refused to go there. My decisions were made and my life was in the here and now, not the there and then. There was a pay phone in town that I used to call home once a week to catch up on the goings-on in a world that now seemed light-years away. Jesse and Jennie were doing fine, just as I knew they would, and Ed was busy taking care of his mother, just as I knew he would. And every time I hung up the phone, I'd walk back to my cabin, feel the sharpness of the winter's cold on my cheeks, look up toward the northern lights washing mysteriously across the sky overhead, and thank whatever power was up there for giving me the life I had.

In the end, Eddie and I divorced. It was nothing like the dramatic, family-rending experiences that most people associate with marital breakups but a simple, rational decision born of financial need: Loretta would receive considerably more social benefits if the government considered Eddie a single head of household caretaker instead of a married one.

As with so many things that had happened to me in my forty-odd years on Earth, it's not how I would have scripted the end of my marriage. But if that was what it would take to make sure that Loretta was taken care of, then that was what we were going to do.

One fucking step at a time. Just one, and in a direction that was right in the moment.

While all of this was going on, I spent my free time feasting on knowledge about trapping in the area from every possible source: where the old cabins were located; who, if anybody, was using them; which animals I should trap and how to handle them once I did. Finally the nine of us were ready, and three months after arriving in the Koyukuk Valley, the dogs and I set out with a sledload of supplies to live a life I'd never seen coming as a girl growing up in Chicago.

Both Coldfoot and Wiseman played significant roles during the gold rush that swept through Alaska and the Yukon in the late 1800s and early 1900s. A gold strike on the Middle Fork of the Koyukuk River and neighboring Nolan Creek saw thousands of people swarm to the area in search of riches. (Coldfoot is actually said to have gotten its name from the would-be prospectors who got "cold feet" once they experienced local conditions and immediately turned tail for home.) The miners who stayed built small cabins along the rivers and creeks as they spread out in ever-widening circles in search of the mother lode. By the 1920s, though, the rush had died and the towns reverted to the tiny communities they've been ever since. Luckily for a first-time trapper, though, the log cabins the early prospectors built remained long after they were gone and—along with dozens of other cabins built by trappers through the ensuing decades—became my homes away from home as I built and worked my trapline. And as with the Chena cabin that saved my life so long ago, the rules of the bush were the same: Cabins not in use were fair game for others to utilize, as long as you left the place in better condition than when you found it and stocked it with a basic supply of essentials such as wood, matches, and canned goods should someone else need to use it.

The first day out of town the dogs and I covered about twenty miles to the first cabin on our line outside Wiseman. Alaska may be small when it comes to people, but the trapping community is even more tight-knit, and once you become part of that select group, you have a pretty good idea of the location of every other trapline in the area. Trappers know that working an area and a population of animals too hard can wreak havoc on the delicate balance of an ecosystem, so they keep their traplines well away from one another. The line I had planned would end up being around a hundred miles long, with traps set every couple of miles depending on terrain and the health of local animal populations.

I spent my first night in the cabin, a low-lying, one-room structure barely tall enough for me to stand up in. It wasn't luxurious by any stretch of the imagination, but its design was purposeful: Lower, smaller cabins meant less interior space to heat and less wood to chop. Plus, I hadn't gone into this venture looking for luxury. Like the other three cabins I'd end up calling my home away from home over the next year and a half, it had a single small window that pointed out toward the open area in front of the cabin where the dogs were kept, which allowed me to keep an eye on them throughout the night.

But night—or sleep, anyway—was still a long way away. I'd spend that first evening the same way I'd go on to spend every other evening I was out working the line: by taking care of the dogs before taking care of myself. After stopping, I'd anchor the sled by securing its snow hook to a nearby tree to make sure it didn't disappear in the night. After settling the dogs and getting them to "line out"—which meant they'd stand stock-still with tension on the gangline that kept them in formation—I'd remove and clean their harnesses, check each animal for possible injury, apply a balm to their pads, even massage the ones that seemed more tired than the others. Then I'd feed them and stake each dog out individually on its own sleeping mat for the cold night ahead. Then, after that job was finally complete, I'd go over the gear one more time, organize my supplies, and head indoors to tend to my own needs.

The cabins that sustained me during my life as a trapper were largely the same when it came to accoutrements: a wood stove, a single counter that served as a combination cooking area/workbench, and, on the far side of the room, a sleeping platform elevated off the ground and covered in a series of animal hides, usually wolf and caribou, to provide insulation and warmth. A battered wooden table and bench or chair filled the middle of the room, and rough-hewn shelves made from local timber lined the walls and held the various supplies and foodstuffs I needed to keep us fed and comfortable. There was little room to spare after I moved in, as I filled each cabin with the various tools, sled parts, traps, and other sundry equipment I needed to make a life on my own feasible. But I soaked up the atmosphere of each one into my soul like a prayer. As I drifted off to sleep each night, the musty smell of a thousand lives seeping from the walls, I knew I had made the right decision. I had become part of the living, breathing history of Alaska.

Over time, the dogs and I fell into a steady and predictable rhythm. I'd scrape the frost off the window and check on the team before putting on a pot of coffee and preparing for the day. Then I'd feed the dogs, strap them into their harnesses, pack up the sled, and, with a loud *Hike!*, hit the trail as my eyelashes started to freeze. Every few miles I'd bring the dogs to a stop, anchor the sled, and wander off to inspect the trap I'd set a couple of days before. If an animal—usually marten, wolverine, muskrat, or fox but occasionally wolf as well—had been caught, I'd remove it and reset the trap and then carry (or drag) the carcass to the sled, where I would lay it inside and move on; empty traps were rebaited. My dogs could run for hours without a break, but I made sure to take care of them, feeding them high-energy snacks along the way. Sometimes our trail would be blocked by a fallen tree or overflow ice from a nearby stream, and I'd have to stop the team to clear our path with an ax, chain saw, or shovel.

I learned a thousand lessons on those trails, each day an education about situations I'd never considered, let alone been taught about. I made so many mistakes I lost count, but with each bumble, I grew a little more. One of the things I hadn't experienced before was just how much wolves *loved* eating dog poop. Winter food supplies can be meager in the Far North, even for such adept hunters as wolves, and apparently I was feeding my dogs so much nutrient-rich food that after they shit it out on the trail as they ran, the wolves came up behind shortly thereafter to clean it up. It wasn't difficult to figure out what was happening. In the wide-open spaces I thought could actually see the wolves emerge slowly behind us, and on all of my return trips, the trail was mysteriously poop-free and crisscrossed with wolf tracks.

Given the wolves' interest in their cousins' waste, I set the few wolf traps I was allowed (wolf trapping is heavily regulated in Alaska) directly behind me and then turned around and picked the animals up on the way back. Once the sled was full, I'd remove the bait from all my traps, pull them up, and head back to Wiseman to deal with the carcasses and their pelts.

Part and parcel of a trapper's life is also a salesperson's life, and on each return trip to town, I would work the animals I'd trapped and then bring their furs to the auctions in Fairbanks. It was a surprisingly high-tech operation for such a traditional vocation: The buyer would scan the pelts with a laser to determine their overall grade and then make an offer for the entire lot. I soon realized my pelts were fetching far less on the market than some other trappers were getting. When I asked what the difference was, a trader opened my eyes to yet another thing I didn't know.

"Well, you're not brain tanning, that's for sure," he said.

As it turns out, brain tanning is a traditional way of tanning animal hides that makes them softer, suppler, and more durable than any other method. Brain tanning involves mixing mashed animal brains with warm water into a slurry, massaging the mixture into a well-soaked hide, followed by a lengthy process of stretching and rewetting. (First Nations peoples usually smoked the hide to make it water resistant and even more durable.) It was time-consuming and labor-intensive, but in the end, the product was far superior and much more valuable than other hand-tanning methods. My initial efforts were piss-poor, but with each successive attempt, I got better. Soon my hides were fetching as much as any other trapper's. My mistakes became fewer and less egregious, and my aptitude grew with each passing week. My bank balance grew accordingly. And then, just as it quickly as it started, my life as a trapper came to an end.

Here's the thing: I can tune out death, human or otherwise. Maybe it was my upbringing, but I have always been comfortable with the fact that death is as much a function of life as living. At the same time, I make sure to *always* respect every life that's been lost, a lesson I learned from both Pat White and Carl the bus driver. So when I found a dead animal in my traps, I spent time with its body, whispered a prayer for its soul, and promised to be a steward for those that remained. The dogs and I ate what we trapped and used as many of the remaining parts as possible.

What I wasn't expecting, though, was the sight that awaited me one spring afternoon.

The traps I used were what's known as "lethal traps," which are designed to kill animals quickly by crushing their neck, spine, or skull, causing instant or near-instant death. It's brutal but effective. But on that morning, I could tell something was off even before I'd walked over to the trap that forever changed my mind about my vocation. The trap had been tripped, but the thing that was in it was too small to make sense. Upon closer inspection, what I saw inside was the single leg of a wolverine, the only thing left behind after the animal had inadvertently stepped in my trap, become fixed in that position, and chewed off its own leg in desperation. I bent over and threw up in the snow.

I knew dying in a trap wasn't the cleanest way to go but had come to grips with the morality of my decision. But knowing that this poor animal had become so desperate that it chewed off its own leg tripped something inside me. Suddenly I was no longer comfortable with the life I had chosen. With hunting, your prey usually doesn't suffer for very long; even after the worst shot you can usually track the animal and bring it down after a couple of hours. They never have to resort to chewing off their own limbs or starving to death. As I lay down later that night in one of my cabins and considered what I'd seen earlier that day, I knew that no amount of freedom or money could make it worthwhile to me anymore. I'll never fault anybody for how they want to live or how they filter the same experiences into their personal being. But suddenly, trapping became not OK to me. I could live my lifestyle without the fur part.

I'd been on the trail for well over a year, a year that had seen me grow in ways I never thought possible. I'd created an inseparable bond with the dogs, filled my bank account to the point where I was feeling pretty comfortable, and reclaimed the soul I'd thought I'd lost back in the Lower 48. What lay ahead was anybody's guess, but when Jesse mentioned that he'd like to spend some time in Alaska with me, the road once again opened up before me in a way I hadn't considered.

The kids and I had kept in close contact after I left, and with time it became apparent that seventeen-year-old Jesse not only missed his mother but also wanted to see for himself the kind of life I was living. So on a brilliant spring afternoon in 2003, he touched down in Fairbanks, where I was waiting to pick him up. After I took him to all my old haunts, we headed up the Haul Road, where he would be introduced to the nuances of my existence.

Jesse took to my way of life instantly. Together we explored the contrasts that springtime in Alaska offered. The ground was still blanketed in its winter coat of snow, rolling off in waves toward the horizon, animal tracks crossing our path in a dizzying web of life and mystery as the sky overhead opened up into the broadest expanse of blue imaginable. He wanted to know everything there was to know about my life: which tracks in the snow indicated what animal, how foxes could manage to smell and successfully hunt the lemmings and voles hiding beneath the snow, how the northern lights occurred, where I'd spent my days and nights while out on the trapline.

But if there was one facet of my existence that Jesse really latched on to, it was the dogs. He formed a bond with the team from the get-go, and within days of his arrival I was teaching him the commands he'd need to run the team himself...which he did. Before he'd head back south to reunite with the father and girlfriend he missed terribly, Jesse would finish the Raven Homeschool program I'd enrolled him in by running the one hundred miles of a nearby dogsled route locals called the Yasuda Trail (named after legendary trader-prospector Frank Yasuda), though it is more commonly known as the Caro-Coldfoot Trail.

On the evening before he was scheduled to fly home, Jesse and I spent one last night walking around Wiseman, eventually returning to the fire pit outside my cabin where we'd started. We'd spent a wonderful few months together, but we both knew that, like his father, his life lay down south.

"You know," he said as he tossed a piece of wood into the fire, "I came up here wondering how you were doing, why you'd chosen this life over the one we all had together. But now I see it. I see who you are here, and I know that this is where you're meant to be. You weren't happy down there; you weren't *you*. But honestly, I can't imagine you anywhere else."

We sat in silence after that, watching the flames dance between us as the night lengthened and the stars appeared overhead. I'd paid a price for my decision to leave… We all do. But I knew in that moment that nothing would ever take me away again.

CHAPTER 5

KAVIK

After Jesse left, spring turned to a glorious Alaskan summer, rivaled by few places on Earth. Though my trapping career had come to an end, the team still needed to be cared for, and we began the off-season training that was vital to keeping the dogs healthy and connected. It was hardly the grueling schedule we'd maintained when we were working the trapline, but on any given day you might find me or other mushers sitting in a wheeled cart as our dogs pulled us down a dusty Wiseman road. Mostly, though, we used the time to socialize and rest. Winters in the far northern reaches of the planet are astoundingly beautiful but exhausting at the same time, and we all relished the opportunity to do a whole lotta nothing.

I was beginning to settle into the simplicity of my summer existence when, on a trip into "town" (Fairbanks) to pick up supplies, I stopped at a local Coldfoot haunt called the Trucker's Table, a restaurant that owed its origins to former Iditarod champion Dick Mackey. Dick had recognized Coldfoot's strategic location midway between Fairbanks and the oil fields in Prudhoe Bay, so back in 1981 he converted an old school bus into a burger stand for truckers traveling the Dalton Highway.

The place had changed substantially over the years (most notably, it was now housed in a permanent structure), but one thing that had remained constant about the Trucker's Table was that it served as a communication hub for people of the region, most of whom invariably stopped in at one point or another. People would either tack a note to a post inside the building or, for those who couldn't get to Coldfoot, give their message to one of the truckers who drove the Haul Road with instructions to affix it to the post or pass the message directly to the intended party. Locals called it "Mukluk Messaging."

I was three bites into a Coldfoot burger when a trucker named Burley (*not* a small man) walked up to my table.

"Hey, Sue. I just put a note on the post for you. Tolbert wants you to call him. Says he's got something he wants to talk to you about. Could mean work, knowing Mike."

Soon thereafter I was on the phone with Mike Tolbert, a man I'd known since I was a kid at North Pole High, and he asked me to babysit his children.

"Hey, Mikey, what's up? I heard you wanted to talk to me."

"Hey there, kiddo, you think can you come in to see me?" he asked. "I want you to do something for me, but I need to talk to you about it. It's kind of…" He paused. "Unique, but right up your alley."

"As a matter of fact, I'm on my way into town right now. I'll come see you tomorrow."

"Perfect. Come as early as you can because it's time sensitive and I'd like to offer it to you first."

Mike wasn't one to waste anyone's time or gas, so I knew whatever he had in mind would be worth hearing about. His office was my first stop the next morning. Shortly after we exchanged pleasantries, Mike told me what was on his mind: He owned a camp on the North Slope and needed someone to look after it for the summer, maybe longer. The caretakers who had worked there for the previous few years suddenly moved on last fall and left him in a big lurch.

Though I'd never been there, I'd heard of the camp and seen it from a distance, an outpost up on the North Slope along the banks of the Kavik River, known to locals as the Kavik River Camp. Mike bought the lease (along with Kavik's buildings and equipment) back in the early '90s in the hopes that a gas line similar to the Alaskan oil pipeline would be built in the gas-rich lands nearby. Such a strike would mean loads of workers coming in, all requiring places to sleep and eat, a need the camp could help accommodate quite nicely. But the gas line had never come to fruition, and

Kavik River Camp had since reverted to hosting the occasional oil and gas professional coming through as well as the scientists and government officials who visited year-round to study everything from rocks to bears to mosquito larvae, the hunters who relished the chance to bring down big Alaskan game, and the adventurers who wanted to explore the nearby Arctic National Wildlife Refuge.

At first, I discounted Mike's offer almost immediately. I had built the kind of life I'd wanted in the Koyukuk Valley and had no interest the in giving it up so soon. Then again, my decision to stop trapping meant I would soon need to find new employment, and Kavik sounded like an adventure the likes of which I had never considered before.

Even for people who have lived their entire lives in Alaska, the North Slope is considered a magical place, for both its natural beauty and the extremeness of its environment. Unlike any place I'd ever lived before, the camp sits square in the middle of the Arctic tundra, that flat, windswept, and unending open expanse of land and low hills dominated by permafrost and a lack of anything taller than a shrub. There, rolling plains stretch for hundreds of miles in every direction, with only rivers like the Kavik to break up the vista. The summers are short and cool, the winters long and brutally cold…even by Alaskan standards. The sun disappears for almost two months in the winter and never sets for the same amount of time in the summer. The North Slope is also the home to a number of dangerous and predatory animals, not the least of which are the grizzly bears that abound in the area. As if that weren't enough, the region is incredibly remote and accessible only by air. Winds can howl with hurricane-like force for days at a time, the temperatures can drop to –80°F and lower, and the weather dictates everything that happens, including life and death.

I was intrigued, though guardedly so.

"Mike," I said. "You know me. I don't do much of anything for just a summer. I've got a bunch of Alaskan malamutes, and it's not so easy to just pick up and move with them. So either I do it year-round or I don't do it at all."

"All right, Sue, I'll leave it to you. But before you get too deep into your deliberations, you have to know that I won't let a woman go in there alone. It's too difficult and too remote."

"Wait… Why?" I asked, my hackles rising ever so slightly at the suggestion that I wasn't good enough. "I've done just fine on my own; I can handle it."

"Sue, *everybody* knows you can handle yourself; that's not the issue," he replied. "But this is an entirely different world than anything you've ever known. You'll be responsible for running and maintaining heavy equipment. Do you know diesel mechanics? Plumbing and electrical? What happens when the generators quit and it's minus seventy-five? Sorry…you go in with a man or you don't go in at all."

I hated that Alaska was still a boys' club, but it was, and Mike had been part of that exclusive society for decades. There was no way he was going to let a woman run Kavik by herself, no matter how capable. And as much as I hated to admit it, I knew he was right. In Alaska, remote lodge work has primarily been the preserve of couples, if only because the physical demands of bush life and associated chores are much better suited to two people than one. Equally important is the fact that hiring a couple eliminates the inevitable sexual tension and potential for harassment that may arise between uncoupled people working together. There were things I had yet to learn how to do, and having a man by my side would only help me on that journey. I'd also heard horror stories about single women running remote camps. In one case, a group of oil workers reportedly landed at a camp, gang-raped the woman who worked there on her own, and left her.

He looked at me for a second and paused. "Don't you have anybody?"

I had no idea what running Mike's camp would mean for my day-to-day existence, but I've never let the unknown stop me from jumping into a new adventure. Winter would be here before I knew it, and Mike needed his answer.

I'll be the first one to admit that I've done a lot of stupid things in my life. Primarily it's because I'm willing to try *anything* that sounds interesting, even if I have no idea how to do the thing in question. Over the years it's meant that I've eventually mastered an awful lot of tasks that I otherwise never would have learned to do, but with that education has come more than my fair share of slip-ups. But what happened in the days after I walked out of Mike Tolbert's office was the absolute pinnacle of Mount Stupidity.

I'd known Joe Henderson on and off for most of my life, a man roughly my age who had spent most of his adult years as a malamute musher and Arctic explorer. Like me, Joe based his dogsled operation out of Wiseman, and we'd gotten to know each other a bit in the time since I'd begun my life as a trapper. Joe loved dogs as much as I did and had an abiding respect for everything that made Alaska the magical place it is. So after calling Eddie and asking if he'd like to join me in this latest adventure (Jennie had gotten married and moved out, but Ed was still looking after his mother and Jesse, so he declined), the second call was to Joe.

I told Joe about Mike's job offer, as well as the caveat of having to go as a couple. I could tell he was as curious about the opportunity as I was, but he said he needed to think about it before making any kind of firm decision. The next day, he called back with an offer of his own, though one I never saw coming.

"So I've been thinking about it," he said, "and I think I have a solution. We can't go to Kavik just as business partners. We'll be alone for months at a time, and the tension between us will be too much. We're both committed to the life we're living. Why not get married and run Kavik together?"

I was struck dumb at his words. *What the living fuck?*

"Well, for one thing, I don't love you," I said.

"You could learn to." He stopped. "Listen, Sue, I know it sounds crazy, but we've always gotten along real well, and I actually think it could work. Plus, we both know the North Slope is *the place* for malamutes to run. We could do the job, run our dogs, and you get the life you want."

I knew Joe had been interested in me for a while; he told me as much over a beer one night in the bar in Coldfoot. I liked the guy, for sure…but marriage was a whole different kettle of fish. On the other hand, I had no other option. I could have tried to find a friend to work the camp with me, but Mike was right: The solitary nature of life at a place like Kavik and the inherent sexual tension that would ensue meant it had to be a couple. Friendships in such conditions simply didn't work.

What the hell, I thought. *People have gotten married for less.*

I called Eddie. He was even more shocked than I was but, as always, trusted my instincts and my process.

"Odd as this sounds," he said, "I understand. You have the call of the wild in your veins, and it seems like this is the only way you're going to get where you want to go. Go get it done, but come back to me on holidays."

He paused for a moment…a breath. Second-guessing himself, maybe?

"Don't you forget about me, Sue," he sighed.

Looking back, I realize that somewhere in the recesses of my tortured brain I was likely still searching for the love I never got as a child. Yes, I'd had love with Eddie, but clearly that hadn't completely filled the hole in my heart created by my childhood and youth. Plus there was a part of me that was painfully old-fashioned: I wasn't about to have sex with anyone unless a ring was involved.

What I forgot, though, is that as much "common sense" as it may have made to marry Joe, marriage should be about love. I forgot what it meant to be emotionally connected to someone, like I was with Eddie. I forgot that if all I wanted was a job, I should have just hired on somewhere else. And in forgetting all of that, I made the biggest mistake in a life filled with them.

Before the week was out, I'd married Joe Henderson in the lobby of a Fairbanks hotel and agreed to run the Kavik River Camp.

In the months after that fateful decision, Joe and I worked furiously to prepare for our life on the North Slope. He flew in a few days ahead of me to set up the dog yard (together we had more than two dozen malamutes), while I drove the dogs and gear in shifts 150 miles north to an area off the Haul Road called Happy Valley. Once an oil camp, Happy Valley also had a short airstrip, which we decided to use as the staging area into Kavik. Under normal circumstances we would have just mushed the dogs in, but there wasn't enough snow cover in the early days of fall and the waterways between Wiseman and Kavik were all still running.

I made the commute to Happy Valley once a day for each of the next four days, eight dogs in the back of the truck with each shuttle. Once there I sedated them and then led them woozily into the bush plane that would take them northeast to Kavik, where Joe was waiting. It was a cumbersome and exhausting undertaking, but the dogs were family; the thought of leaving them behind never crossed my mind.

On the fifth day, it was finally time for me to make the trip to Kavik. I was buzzing with excitement as the pilot and I loaded the last of my gear onto the de Havilland Beaver. Before me lay a road full of adventure, an arrow shot directly into the heart of the wildest, most remote part of the state. I had saved my own life in a cabin in the wilderness outside Fairbanks, put myself through school in a wall tent, and shared space with the ghosts of countless trappers and miners who had come before me, but this was something entirely different altogether.

As the Beaver ascended from the gravel airstrip, the Haul Road stretched like a gray ribbon toward the oil fields to the north as we climbed steadily over the low hills as rivers named and unnamed slashed lines of blue against the green carpet of the valley floors below. It's an awe-inspiring landscape, no matter how many times you've flown it, walked it, hunted it, or ridden it on a sled behind a team of dogs. There were few signs of civilization below. No towns, no buildings, no vehicles. Just the land and the critters that called it home.

After about an hour, the pilot banked the plane and the Kavik River Camp appeared below, a roughshod cluster of buildings and structures that offered stark contrast against the wilderness that crowded around it on all sides. Alongside the camp, the Kavik River meandered in lazy loops through braided channels, its waters pale with glacial silt. I took a deep breath and smiled. A new home and a new adventure awaited.

But as the plane made its final approach to the runway, I could tell something was off. I'd seen northern camps before, and they're utilitarian at best, a jumble of trailers, equipment, and parts cobbled together to create a functional unit. But the state of the camp that awaited me that day was far worse than anything I'd ever imagined. I knew it hadn't been looked after for a while, but Kavik looked like hell.

Never in my life have I doubted my own strength. Ever. I'm tough as fuck. I've seen and done things that lots of people shake their heads at. But I'm not completely devoid of emotion either, and sometimes a girl just has to cry. So when I got out of the plane and surveyed the full scope of my new reality, I broke down.

The place was more than simply abandoned by its last caretakers; it had been neglected for a *very* long time. Garbage was heaped in random piles, and the main dump site—an area at the back of camp I would come to call The Boneyard—was well over twenty feet tall. There were signs of bear and other animal activity *everywhere*, and it appeared as though nothing had been maintained for years. As I stood there beside Joe and took in the magnitude of the scene, doubt began to carom through my head. *Can we actually do this? How did it get so bad? What the hell are we gonna do with this mess?*

The clouds were dropping quickly—a common autumn phenomenon on the North Slope—so once we emptied the plane of all the remaining gear, the pilot took off quickly before he was stuck at Kavik for an indeterminate period of time. If there was one thing I'd learned during my Alaskan life, it's that weather is king… and nobody knows that better than a bush pilot.

Still in shock, I made my way to Kavik's dining hall and kitchen—a Quonset-style tent about thirty feet long and fifteen feet across, with a heavy vinyl fabric pulled tight over a frame of successive steel ribs—to gather my thoughts, assess the situation, and plan my next steps. The inside of the building was also an unmitigated disaster. Joe had focused most of his energy on getting the dogs settled, and it looked as though the only things that had lived in the dining hall in recent months were the animals that had torn through *everything*. There was scat everywhere: fox, wolverine, even bear. The long dining tables inside the room had been overturned, and the room's two "couches"—sheets of plywood perched on oil drums that had been cut in half—were peppered with shit. All the water lines in the place had obviously frozen and ruptured over the previous winter; muddy pools of water had spread across the buckled and molding floor.

As I stood there dumbstruck, reality hit me. Joe and I had committed ourselves to the job, the dogs and all our gear had already been unloaded, and the plane was on its way back to town. Overwhelmed, I walked outside to catch my breath and come to terms with my new life.

Stunned, I wandered toward the airstrip a few hundred yards away. The low clouds had now settled closer to the ground and turned into a thick fog; it was hard to see more than fifty feet in any direction. I dropped my head to my chest and sighed. I had built a beautiful life for myself in the Koyukuk Valley, running dogs and spending all my time outdoors. I'd built up my bank account, forged a strong bond with my animals, and shed the weight of the life in the Lower World that had almost crushed me. And now I'd given it all up…and for what?

My reverie was interrupted by a sound, something that made the hair on the back of my neck stand up. I looked to see where the noise was coming from, but the fog was too thick. As I stood there, frozen, the noise grew progressively louder until I was finally able to identify it: the sound of four very large paws thundering across the ground and the telltale *whoof, whoof, whoof* of a bear on the move.

Like a brown bolt of lightning, a massive grizzly appeared out of the soup and charged toward me at breakneck speed. The bear was beside me before I could breathe (Alaskan grizzly bears can hit speeds of forty miles an hour over short distances) and swung one of its plate-sized forepaws at me as it raced past. Mercifully, it missed and then disappeared into the fog as quickly as it had appeared, but before it did I was able to catch a glimpse of the red tag in its right ear.

Bears had been a part of my life since I was a girl, but that was *not* the welcoming committee I was counting on. Shock turned to adrenaline, and seconds later I was sprinting back to the dining hall, where I threw myself on the makeshift oil-drum couch. I didn't know it at the time, but I'd just met Mardy, Kavik's resident female alpha bear who, in the years ahead, would become a neighbor and nemesis like none I'd ever known.

For the first time in my life, going back on my word was a very real option. Mike would understand and certainly pay to fly us and our gear back to Wiseman. At the same time, though, I'd never backed down from a challenge, and Kavik was most certainly that.

Then something clicked. The close call with Mardy engaged the part of my personality that thrives on challenges and refuses to accept defeat. Why did the astronauts choose to go to the moon when death was a very real possibility? Because it takes a unique mentality to look into the darkness and still want to see what's on the other side. Plus, I'd given Mike my word that I would stay. And at the end of the day, as daunting and scary as Kavik had become, my word was everything.

At that moment, the path forward became clear. I began to look at Kavik through a different set of lenses. No longer was the camp an unmitigated disaster, but a diamond in the rough that needed me to help it realize its full potential. I began to do the work in my head, lay out the necessary steps to make the camp what it could one day be. And then I walked outside and yelled as loud as I could into the fog, "Fuck you, bear! Come and get me… I'll be waiting!"

I turned back into the dining hall, turned the tables upright, and started to clean up. How do you eat an elephant? One bite at a time.

Even though Joe and I were living in a what could only be described as an oversized tent in the far northern regions of Alaska, we enjoyed more modern conveniences than Kavik's location otherwise dictated. There was heat from a series of stoves that ran on jet fuel, electricity from a handful of diesel-powered generators, running water from a collection of large tanks that we could fill before the river froze, and even a bunkhouse that had been converted into a shower room. We weren't completely cut off from human contact, either. We had radio communication; eventually we even got internet. But it was the bush pilots who used Kavik as a refueling stop who kept us abreast of what was happening in the outside world as well as the recent history of the camp.

Seems the people who were running Kavik before Joe and I arrived realized that the garbage they left everywhere attracted scores of bears, and bears attract hunters. So rumor had it that they started to quietly make it known that a person could come to Kavik for a guaranteed bear kill in exchange for some cash on the down-low. Now, baiting a grizzly bear on the North Slope is illegal, so it didn't take a brain surgeon to realize that the couple likely abandoned the place in such a rush because they'd been found out. Either way, they did nothing to close up shop before they left, just chartered the quickest plane they could find and disappeared.

In the meantime, Joe and I had become just another entry in a long list of creatures to call the Kavik River valley home, beginning with the First Nations people who had hunted in the area for millennia. They named the place *Kavik*, which comes from the Inupiaq word meaning *wolverine*, which are abundant in the river valley and surrounding land.

The Inupiat weren't the only people to recognize how special a place the valley is. Early visitors from the U.S. Geological Survey talked about the uniqueness of the Kavik watershed, including its plant life, mineral content, and incredible variety of animal species. Aside from the bears and wolverines, there are caribou, fox, and wolves, and the valley also provides habitat for wintering moose and musk oxen.

Yet not everyone who passed through the region was drawn to Kavik for its plants and animals: They also came here for what they could find *under* the ground. As far back as the 1940s, the area was considered a "place of interest" by the U.S. government for its natural resource potential. Go back even further to the turn of the twentieth century, and you'll encounter a little-known explorer named Ernest de Koven Leffingwell, who spent parts of nine years in the Arctic between 1901 and 1914. During that time, Leffingwell covered an insane amount of Alaskan territory (he made thirty-one trips by dogsled or small boat) and created the first accurate map of large parts of the Arctic coastline. More importantly for Kavik, Leffingwell accurately identified the oil potential of the North Slope, predicting it would one day be one of the world's largest oil and gas reserves.

He was right, and once the multinational oil companies caught on and figured out a way to extract the resources from the ground, Kavik was on the map. At the height of that activity, there were approximately 1,500 people living and working at the camp, making it the biggest of its kind on the North Slope. Rock crushers worked day and night to feed the endless thirst for gravel that was piled onto the tundra in makeshift roads stretching toward remote drilling sites. Even now, these gravel trails crisscross the tundra all the way to Canada, though they're harder to spot because of the sedges and bushes that have grown up around them over the ensuing years. Yet without any road connecting Kavik to the south, the real lifeline of the place came via the air, so the Kavik airstrip was born. A mile long, it's big enough to land some of the largest aircraft on Earth, like the C-130 Hercules planes that once shuttled heavy equipment in and out.

The place was abuzz with activity in those days. Machinery churned ceaselessly; a series of lights kept the runway lit through the darkest days of winter; there was even a control tower to ensure the safety of the constant flow of aircraft. Gas was abundant, and business was good. At one point, there were as many as seven operational gas wells in and around Kavik. Then, as quickly as it started, it stopped.

Those same multinationals figured out there was more cash in Prudhoe Bay's oil than in Kavik's gas, and almost as quickly as they were built, the natural gas wells were capped and production came to a screeching halt. Equipment, including the rock crushers, was burned, abandoned, buried, or moved north to the oil fields. With no fresh gravel, the roads all fell into disrepair and were slowly reclaimed by the elements. I would drive those trails in a quad for the next two decades, but they were riddled with bumps and holes, and the bushes had grown around them as nature slowly reclaimed itself.

Yet under it all, the gas remained. The Kavik gas field, as it became known, is still the largest "stranded" natural gas field of its kind. A handful of companies have come and gone over the past thirty years or so as mapping and extraction techniques improved, but the big rush—the one that Mike Tolbert was hoping would be the next boom—never happened.

Despite the complete lack of consideration on my part, my relationship with Joe wasn't horrible. It wasn't great by any stretch...but at least it wasn't horrible. He spent most of his time with the dogs, while I focused on the camp and the laundry list of things that needed to be done to whip it into shape. We occasionally did things together, but that's largely where it ended. So as the Arctic fall quickly turned to winter, I had lots of time to be alone with my thoughts.

In those moments, I often drifted to images of my family down in Portland, wisps of memory from a life that now seemed light-years away. But blessing or curse, I've never been one to dwell on the past, and at the moment, Kavik was front and center in my consciousness. I began by addressing the garbage that had been accumulating for decades, initially by burning it in the 1940s/'50s-era industrial-grade incinerator at the back end of camp. But the larger pieces of equipment and hazardous materials needed to be flown the 350-odd miles to Fairbanks to be disposed of properly. Luckily, both Mike Tolbert and I had good relationships with the people at Everts Air in Fairbanks, and every time one of their planes landed at Kavik with guests or supplies, they let us load up some junk for the return trip.

We continued in earnest with Kavik's restoration as fall turned to winter, which was like none I'd ever experienced. I was accustomed to the cold and the dark, but Kavik's was colder and darker than anything I'd ever known. But what made my first North Slope winter decidedly more unique than any I'd lived through was the wind. At its worst, the wind would start building somewhere out over the Arctic Ocean, roll over the northern plains, and then reach hurricane force by the time it barreled over Kavik. And in a camp littered with the forgotten by-products of its former industrial self, that meant there were countless objects that could quickly morph from decorations into projectiles. Occasionally, important things even got taken away by the wind, never to be seen again. We quickly learned that the first lesson of a Kavik winter was to secure everything to the ground or store it away, lest we never see it again.

I tried to stay inside when those storms were raging, primarily because I didn't want to lose my head to a random piece of sheet metal I had yet to uncover, but sometimes duty called me into the heart of the gale. In those moments, when it was minus sixty degrees and I couldn't see more than a foot in front of my face for the sheets of snow that blew sideways all around me, I reminded myself that I was living the life I'd asked for all along. All those times in the Lower World when I felt my soul being slowly compressed into something hard and dead, this was what I had wanted. Kavik was the biggest challenge of my life, but I went to bed every night with an abiding sense of satisfaction and peace. I was home.

Joe and I continued that way for the next eight months or so. He focused most of his energy on the dogs and continued to explore the North Slope on trips that would take him away from camp for days and sometimes weeks at a time. I spent almost every waking hour getting Kavik back into shape. First came the cleanup, but as those efforts began to bear fruit, I also began to renovate and rebuild the camp's various physical structures, from the scat-riddled dining hall to the building that housed the generators and other heavy equipment, which we dubbed the "gen shed."

In between, there was the completely foreign task of running one of the northernmost bed-and-breakfasts on Earth, as the occasional scientists, hunters, and ecotourists who showed up needed to be housed in one of our many bunkhouse trailers and then fed, debriefed, and pointed in the right direction for whatever activity they were pursuing. The responsibilities were as vast as they were diverse. Each morning began with a safety assessment of the camp's critical systems, including generators, fuel levels, water and plumbing, and communication equipment. From there I'd check on the weather to prepare for any potential disruptions that may have been headed our way. On the days when guests were in camp, I'd then start preparing breakfast, sometimes for as many as twenty people. Then the real work started.

There was maintenance of essential infrastructure (water and waste systems, heating, and cabins); repairs and troubleshooting; runway clearance and upkeep; ordering fuel, food, and supplies; wildlife monitoring and mitigation; coordinating aircraft arrivals and departures; bookings, guest inquiries, and reservations;

and communication with local authorities, emergency services, and suppliers. Then, when evening finally rolled around, it was time to cook dinner and host the guests, each of whom apparently wanted to be regaled with a scotch and a story of Alaskan adventure. When dinner was finished and the dishes cleaned, I'd perform a final safety check and secure Kavik for the night, once again making sure our four-legged neighbors were staying well-enough away…before planning for the next day's activities. Add to this the clear and present danger of a rapid, violent change in weather that could bring the entire system to its knees, and it's easy to see why I felt overwhelmed at times. Kavik represented a life in the greatest natural playground on Earth, but every day offered a series of logistical challenges the likes of which I'd never known.

My emotions went on a roller-coaster ride of similar magnitude and diversity. Depending on the time of day or year, I felt overwhelmed and stressed, empowered and fulfilled, isolated, resourceful, excited, and downtrodden. But more than anything, the single primary emotion that I felt in living at the Kavik Camp was contentment. And then it all blew up.

Jennie had her first baby not long after I moved to Kavik, but my grandson's start on life was anything but smooth. In fact, as our first winter at Kavik turned to spring, Jen called me with the news that no grandmother ever wants to hear: Nathan had been diagnosed with cancer. Gutted, I chartered the first plane I could and made my way down to Portland, where they were living; Joe would run Kavik in my absence. It was an important time for me: Not long before, Mike Tolbert had agreed to transfer Kavik's lease over to me and sell me the associated buildings and equipment. When the transaction was completed in a few days' time, I'd be Kavik's sole owner. (Joe wanted no part of ownership.) Since I had no idea how long I'd be gone, Joe agreed to handle the transaction in my absence.

The night before I left, I sat down with Joe. "The sale is going to close in a few days. I've added your name to my accounts so you can fulfill the purchase agreement. If there are any issues, you can take care of them while I'm gone."

"OK, not a problem," he replied.

Seven weeks later I returned, but as soon as the plane touched down, I knew something was wrong. Joe wasn't waiting by the runway, and the dogs were gone. His dogs *and* my dogs. I checked the camp for any sign of them, but there was nothing. But Joe and the dogs weren't the only things that were gone. So was just about everything else of value around camp.

Then the greatest insult of all. With the walls rapidly closing in around me, I hopped onto my online banking to check the status of my accounts. I guess I shouldn't have been surprised at that point, but the sight that met my eyes knocked the wind out of me nonetheless. The account to which I'd added Joe—the one that held my life savings and was supposed to pay for Kavik—was empty. He had taken every penny. I was forty-four years old, had a driver's license that listed latitude and longitude coordinates as my address, and owned little more than the clothes on my back.

Months later Joe and I would meet in Fairbanks to finalize the divorce. Walking into the courtroom that day, I felt a mix of anger and sadness but, more than anything, a hollow kind of relief. I hadn't spoken with him since he had vanished from Kavik, and the betrayal sat like a stone in my chest. When I saw him sitting there, across the sterile expanse of the courtroom, I wondered if he'd changed at all, but his expression was unreadable. When our eyes finally met, I searched for some indication of regret, shame, or maybe even defiance but was instead met with avoidance. He couldn't hold my gaze for long but shifted in his chair uncomfortably, pretending to study the paperwork in front of him.

The judge's voice brought me back to the moment. I had hoped I'd get some of my money back but knew my fate was sealed when the judge said, "Sue, you put him on your accounts willingly, so there's nothing we can do. We can empathize and sympathize. But legally, we can't do a thing."

At first, I wanted to put up more of a fight. I wanted to hurt the man who had somehow decided that being married to me was reason enough to destroy my life. But in the end, I lowered my hackles and let it all go. For better or worse, mine is a life that is firmly rooted in the present, and all I wanted to do at that point was let go of the pain and move forward with my life. And that, at least, felt like a victory.

One step at a time. You'll figure it out.

After I walked away from the court, the first thing I did was go see Mike Tolbert. Mike knew what had happened with Joe and the money, but I'd told him all along that I was going to get it back. Now I had to break the news to him: I had no money and no man to help me run the camp. But that didn't mean I was going down without a fight.

"Here's what I can do," I said. "I'll work for you for the next five, six years. You take 80 percent of my wages and put them in the kitty, apply them to the purchase of the camp. At the end of that time, I'll pay you the balance. Add in sweat equity and you actually have a damned good offer…but that's the best I can do."

He looked at me, silent. He had known me almost all my life, and if anybody knew what I was capable of doing, it was Mike. Still, it was clear from the look on his face that he had his doubts. Kavik was different, and we both knew it. Eventually, Mike spoke.

"Do you really think you can do it on your own?" he asked.

I considered his question before offering the most logical answer I could muster. "Well, I don't know that I *can't*," I said. "And right now, that's all I can tell you." Mike looked at me long and hard, his face dead serious. I caught my breath, prepared myself for the ax that was about to fall: My dream was about to end. Then he exhaled and shook his head as he stood up and held up his hand.

"Well, if there's anyone on this goddamn planet who can do it on their own, it's you, Susie Moore."

I exhaled and then jumped out of my seat to meet his hand in mine. "You goddamn got that right," I said.

Kavik was all mine, and I wasn't going to let anyone take it away from me.

CHAPTER 6

FRIENDS AND FOES

I returned to Kavik as a single woman, the newest lone wolf in the vast and complex ecosystem that defined the North Slope. I was alone but never lonely, challenged but not crippled. And yet it was difficult at times to not feel massively insignificant in the grand panoply of life unfolding all around me. In a world where I was literally the only person living for hundreds of miles in any direction, without a shred of humanity or even the thinnest safety net to bail me out of trouble, Mother Nature ruled *all.*

I had accepted that reality many years before and tried once again to find my place within it. I knew where I fit in a life on the Chena road, had carved a niche for myself and my dogs in the Koyukuk and Chandalar River valleys. However, the art of living alone on the North Slope and being the caretaker of a self-sufficient village of bunkhouses and associated equipment while simultaneously playing host to random guests and airplanes would take some time to learn. But that's exactly what I intended to do.

Along the way, my struggles were primal, dangerous: living in a glorified tent a handful of miles from the Arctic Ocean; minus-one hundred-degree wind chills; losing my only source of electricity for weeks in the middle of winter. It was Mother Nature herself making sure that Sue Aikens clearly understood the meaning of death. But as much as I abided her constant presence, I refused to yield my ground. She could have everything else, but Kavik was *mine*.

At the same time, I reveled in the things that *didn't* accompany my life. I wasn't burdened by the demands of society or a nagging spouse. I didn't malign my commute, my boss, or my job. I didn't worry about local crime, national politics, or how much time I was spending watching television. When problems invariably arose, I was on my own to figure them out. Sometimes I did so gracefully; other times I floundered my way through and made massive, stupid mistakes along the way. But with each day that passed, I grew in confidence, if only for the fact that I was *surviving*. I was living alone at Kavik and still had very little knowledge of diesel mechanics (though admittedly a bit more than when I first arrived), but I was still alive.

I rejoiced in the freedoms that Kavik offered. I woke up when I wanted, slept when I felt like it. Those rhythms took on their own personality in the dark of winter, a two-month period between late November and late January where the sun never rose above the horizon at all and the lightest it got was a purple-haze twilight that brushed the sky for a few hours each day. But when the darkest days of winter descended in late December, it was just me and the stars above. In those times, where the visual clues between day and night blurred to the point where they were virtually indistinguishable from one another, my body began to set its own schedule. I'd sleep for inordinately long periods of time, sometimes as long as thirty-six hours straight, followed by periods of wakefulness of the same length. With no schedule and nobody to answer to but myself, I redefined the rules of my daily existence.

Yet with Joe gone I also felt an increased sense of urgency to build an intimate knowledge of the area around camp, a step I saw as essential to ensuring my well-being in the years to come. If I was going to survive I needed to catalog the presence of every possible opportunity and threat in the immediate vicinity. What edible plants and shrubs grew nearby? When did the bears awaken from their winter slumber? What sources of fresh water were there? How many wolves were in the pack that roamed the nearby hills? How much would the river flood when it broke up in the spring? These and a thousand other questions needed answering, and the only way to get the insights I sought was to get as close to the land as I could. So as soon as the sun returned, I walked.

To the extent that a weather forecast could accurately predict the day's conditions, I only picked the most promising ones for my forays into the heart of the North Slope. Blizzards in that part of the world can whip up with deadly speed, and I knew that to become disoriented in a blinding Arctic whiteout while traveling on foot away from camp could mean my death. So I made sure the skies were blue and the sun shining before I headed out the door, my backpack filled with such essentials as a GPS, a satellite phone, a thermos of hot coffee, some snacks, a rifle slung over my shoulder, and a .44 on my hip.

Then I walked away from camp, either north alongside the Kavik River toward the hills that separated me from the Arctic Ocean, east toward the Canning River valley, south toward the Brooks Range, or west across the Kavik and out into the tundra. But no matter which direction I went, it wasn't long before the stillness of the land consumed me, the only sounds the squeak of my boots on the Styrofoam-like snow as the low sun grazed the horizon and painted the palette of white around me in an ever-changing mosaic of long, slender shadows.

The tundra of Alaska's North Slope is a marvelous thing, quite unlike any other ecosystem on Earth, a vast, open expanse large enough to comfortably accommodate the state of Idaho with room to spare. Around me, the land was dotted with the low shrubs and frozen tussocks that occasionally poked through a mantle of snow that was surprisingly hard in places, the product of an endless battering of wind that locked it into wave-like ridges known as sastrugi. In other places, the snow was oddly fragile and dotted with fox prints zigzagging in every direction, evidence of their nightly hunts for such prey as lemmings, voles, or ptarmigans. Willow shrubs and dwarf birches were stripped of their leaves, skeletal outlines against the snow, wind-scoured rocks dotted with lichens a reminder of summer's fleeting abundance and another potential food source in a pinch.

Occasionally, I came across larger sets of tracks, mostly caribou and wolf, sometimes wolverine. While much of the wildlife around camp migrated or hibernated for the winter, I was certainly not alone. Caribou were not a threat, but I needed to assess their movement patterns because they were a vital source of food and fur. Wolf tracks represented an entirely different kind of neighbor, though. I knew wolf attacks on humans were exceedingly rare, but that didn't mean I could take my safety for granted, especially now that I was on my own.

As the day progressed, I climbed one of the many hills near Kavik to get a better view of the horizon. Below me, the frozen Kavik River shimmered in the weak daylight, the gray peaks of the Brooks Range loomed mysteriously in the distance. The wind was stronger at the hilltop, biting through even the multiple layers I wore. Most of the weather at Kavik comes from the north, so I scanned the horizon intently for any signs of a potential weather shift, such as changes in cloud formations or wind direction, which can signal an impending storm. Satisfied I was safe, I sat down, poured myself a cup of coffee, and soaked up the fullness of my surroundings.

The solitude was as deep as any I'd ever known, everything basted in a silence as heavy as it was comforting. I felt small—a mere dot of living flesh and bones in an unyielding moonscape—but profoundly connected nonetheless. Light was in short supply, so I knew that no matter how clear the day I couldn't linger too much longer for risk of needing to find my way back in the dark. I had a headlamp, but the last thing I wanted to do was come face-to-face with a pack of wolves in the Arctic night. So as the sun began to sink hastily toward the horizon and bathe the sky in violet and pink, I hurried down the hill and back toward camp. The air was so cold it burned my lungs with every breath; my eyelashes were covered with a fuzzy rime of frost. If there was ever a place more beautiful and powerful than Kavik, I hadn't yet come across it.

Later, after I'd fired up the heater inside the dining hall (where I'd partitioned off a separate ten-foot-by-ten-foot section to serve as my bedroom), I cooked myself a simple meal of pasta with caribou Bolognese and lay back on the couch. My dogs were gone, my bank account empty, Eddie and the kids thousands of miles away. But as I drifted in and out of sleep, I realized that no matter how difficult life might be at times, no matter how vulnerable I was, no matter how long it would be before I was able to enjoy the trappings of "civilized" life once again, I was home. I had committed my heart and my soul to Kavik, and I was going to throw everything I had into it.

I got up off the couch and wandered outside in my slippers. It was minus forty-six degrees. Overhead, the aurora danced across the sky in ribbons of green and purple, a final gift from the tundra before the day ended.

For years, people have asked me how I've been able to handle a life of such *loneliness*, a word I've never understood, if only for the fact that the math doesn't add up. For me, being alone has never equated to being lonely. As much as I love people and occasionally relish their company, I am fine living by myself for extended periods of time. Plus, life in Alaska had taught me that while humans may be far away, the animals never are.

At Kavik, my most constant companions were the foxes—primarily red foxes, though occasionally the snow-white Arctic foxes—that made their homes in the folds of land around camp. They were leery of me, perhaps even scared, but with time they allowed me to draw ever closer as they realized I wasn't a threat to their existence. I observed their movements, delicate yet purposeful, as they danced on a razor's edge of survival.

The foxes were easy to spot, bright orange slashes against a white backdrop, bushy tails trailing behind them like bursts of flame in a frozen landscape. Yet as playful as they seemed, they were also deadly hunters. I watched in awe as their ears swiveled instinctively when they caught the slightest sound of potential prey beneath the snow, cocked their head, and pounced, a perfectly timed dive that shattered the crust to reveal an unsuspecting vole or lemming hidden below.

At first, I kept my distance. The foxes had no idea who or what I was, and an animal's survival in the wilds of Alaska is the product of its cunning and wariness. Yet with time, my presence became familiar to them, one of the few things that remained unchanged in their territory. At first, the foxes approached hesitantly as they tested the boundaries of our relationship, the Arctic silence broken by the faint sound of their paws padding over snow. In the months to come they'd return, each time a bit closer, each time studying me with a gaze that warmed my soul. Meanwhile, I spent more and more time sitting quietly on the outskirts of camp, letting them observe me as much as I did them. On windless days, their chirps and barks punctuated the air, high-pitched, almost playful sounds of them communicating with one another as they explored. Slowly, they began to associate me not as a threat, but just another neutral fixture in camp.

For almost twenty years, those foxes would be my constant companions. Not pets, not friends, but kindred spirits in a shared life. I watched them build their dens, have their babies, and die in the frigid Arctic air. When I was fixing something outside, I noticed how they moved closer, as though drawn by curiosity. And yet I never lost sight of the fact that as cute and fuzzy as they may have seemed, at the end of the day they were still wild animals that would always revert to instinct over adulation. I knew that if I found myself lying incapacitated on the tundra, they'd be the first ones to make me into a Sueburger. That said, the foxes were an inspiration to me. They reminded me—as they've done every day since—that as dark as the world may seem at times, life persists with grace and tenacity, shaped by land and light. And every day I admired their resilience, their ability to endure the dark months and return with purpose and wonder.

And then one evening, in the dim glow of a late winter twilight, one fox, bolder and more confident than its peers, came into camp and approached me closer than ever. It stared at me curiously, head cocked to one side before sniffing the air and circling cautiously as though it recognized me as part of the rhythm of the place. It barked, a sound so sharp and alive against the silence that it startled me to laughter. I crouched down to get an eye-level look at the fox, but it neither approached nor backed away, just continued to eye me curiously.

"Hi, Baby," I said.

While the foxes began to evolve into something more akin to roommates than neighbors, the bears that lived in and around Kavik remained a constant threat to my existence, the likes of which I'd never experienced before. In the years leading up to my tenure at Kavik, the grizzly population had reached frightening proportions, largely the product of my predecessors' apparent lack of interest in disposing of their waste. And while my efforts to clean up the place had begun to address the issue, the bears still outnumbered me by a large margin. Every day I was aware of my precarious place on the food chain. And of the many bears that frequented Kavik, none proved to be as persistent and unsettling as Mardy, four hundred pounds of piss and vinegar that stretched seven feet long from tip to tail.

I'd seen Mardy (the name given to her by the state's wildlife troopers) on and off ever since she'd taken a swipe at me on the runway my first day in camp; the telltale red tag in her ear made it easy to identify her. She largely limited her forays into camp to The Boneyard, but recently I'd seen her tracks all over, including the area just outside the dining hall.

One evening in late May, I was reading in bed when the silence of the night was shattered by a sound I can only liken to a Volkswagen Beetle being peeled open by the world's largest can opener. It's not a sound most people are familiar with, but I'd actually heard it once before, during a family trip to Yellowstone National Park in the '70s, a time when visitors treated the place more like a game farm than a natural habitat.

On one afternoon during that trip, my stepfather Joe was driving a few cars behind a Volkswagen Beetle full of teenagers who entertained themselves by feeding marshmallows to a black bear. At some point, the kids must have decided to save some treats for their campfire that night, so they rolled up the windows, a decision the bear clearly disagreed with. After contemplating the vehicle for a few seconds, the bear decided that since the marshmallows were no longer coming *out* to her, she was going to go *in* to get them. With a flick of her forepaw, she cut through the outer layer of metal on the car and began to peel it open. The kids sped away before anything else could happen, but the sound was forever etched in my memory. It's a sound I never thought I'd hear again, though... until that night.

I threw on my clothes, grabbed the nearest rifle, and started yelling as I walked tentatively outside the dining hall door and into the twilight. There, startled and running awkwardly down the stairs of the trailer right outside my door—a trailer I used for storing most of the camp's nonperishable food items—was Mardy. I fired a couple of warning shots into the ground behind her, and she lumbered off through the willows, down toward the river, and away from camp.

With Mardy a safe distance away, I assessed the damage. The door of the food-storage trailer—about six inches of insulated foam wrapped in a stainless-steel shell—had been peeled open from top to bottom. Thankfully she never made it inside or the damage would have been much more substantial. Curious as to what drew her attention, I walked inside and took stock of the trailer's contents, a treasure trove of treats for a hungry bear, all laid out neatly on the rows of shelves inside. Since taking over the camp I'd been meticulous about keeping everything inside the trailer sealed and airtight, but when I got to a back corner, I saw what had likely drawn Mardy's attention: a jar of molasses, a remnant of my predecessors' time, had shattered in the cold, its contents slowly oozing across the floor like tar.

Grizzly bears have an incredibly acute sense of smell, one of the most powerful in the animal kingdom. In fact, not only does a bear boast olfactory capabilities that are more than two thousand times more sensitive than a human's, their sense of smell is significantly more sensitive than even that of dogs, including breeds like bloodhounds. While bloodhounds possess about three hundred million olfactory receptors, bears like Mardy are estimated to have about two billion of them. On top of that, the relative portion part of a bear's brain dedicated to smell is approximately five times bigger than that of a bloodhound. In short, they are extraordinarily specialized when it comes to smelling. So the molasses on the floor would have been calling to Mardy, even at a distance of fifteen to twenty miles away.

So instead of heading back to bed, I turned my attention to cleaning up the mess. After ten minutes of scrubbing with hot water, I rubbed it down with bleach in a desperate attempt to mask the scent. I knew nothing would completely dull the aroma for Mardy but had to do as much as I could to make camp less attractive to her. She'd become habituated over the years to the fact that Kavik represented an easy food source, and I needed to do everything I could to disabuse her of that notion.

Fixing the trailer door was a whole different kind of challenge, with the nearest hardware store almost five hundred miles away in Fairbanks and no road in between. With night falling, I retreated to the relative safety of the dining hall, but as soon as it was light the next morning, I made my way back to the camp's workshop, where I bolted a few pieces of wood across the damaged parts of the door.

It wasn't pretty, but my handiwork would have to suffice until I could get more permanent materials flown in. In the meantime, all I could do was hope I'd done enough to keep Mardy from coming back, though I knew it was a pipe dream. For a bear, the rules of existence are simple but rigid. *Smell something to eat, go get it...no matter what's in the way.* In other words, Mardy got what Mardy wanted, and short of shooting her, there wasn't much I could do.

Luckily, my patchwork efforts seemed to work...for a while, anyway. Mardy's forays into camp became less and less frequent. I saw her, of course, though usually from a safe distance as I sat on a snow machine watching her roam the tundra, feeding on the roots, plants, and berries that comprised the majority of her diet. But a few years later, Mardy became more interested in Kavik than she'd ever been before, and her interest almost killed me.

As the years passed, I became incredibly adept at picking up on the subtle changes in sound that occurred around Kavik, both man-made and natural. The generator dominated the soundscape when it was running, but when I turned it off at night, the noises of the natural world filled in the blanks: the wind whooshing across the tundra, the trills and whistles of a group of snow buntings, the snorts of a herd of caribou as they crossed a nearby hillside, the gentle burbles of the river as it wound its way in braided channels down below the camp. Eventually, my sense of hearing became even more acute. I could sense the generator misfiring before the sound reached my ears. I could hear an animal crossing the river, could tell by sound of the splash if it was a bear or a caribou, even the direction it was traveling.

It was fall hunting season, early September 2006. There were a handful of guests in camp, all hunters, all of whom had gone to bed in their trailers. Having just finished my evening's chores and shut things down for the night, I retreated to my makeshift bedroom in the dining hall where I was beginning to doze off when I heard that different sort of sound that always caught my attention. Only this time, the hairs on the back of my neck stood on end when I realized I was hearing the *squish squish squish* of grizzly paws coming across the river.

It was unlikely anyone else in camp heard the noise. The trailers are fairly soundproof, their doors beefy enough to not let much sound pass. I, on the other hand, had only about an eighth-inch of vinyl tent wall separating me from the outside world. Moments later, the sound changed again, the *squish* replaced by the sound of long claws coming up the bank and then clacking against the gravel. As the sounds drew closer, I was at full attention, now sitting up in bed and considering my next move. Did I need to go outside and scare the bear away? My answer came when the claws-on-gravel noise, now accompanied by heavy sniffing and breathing, stopped outside my tent, directly behind my head. I leapt out of bed mere seconds before a three-inch claw sliced through the tent wall, followed by the entire dinner-plate-size paw of a full-grown grizzly, followed by Mardy's head.

Now to paint the complete picture…when it's still warm outside, I sleep in the buff. Only when full-blown winter sets in and outside temperatures plummet does buff get replaced with clothing. But on that night, I was sleeping in my altogether.

With Mardy beginning to push herself through the ever-widening tear in the side of the tent, I had no time to do anything but ram my feet in the top of my XTRATUF boots sitting at the foot of my bed, grab the closest rifle (I *always* slept with at least one gun within arm's reach of the bed), and run like hell. Why putting on the boots made sense while the rest of me was butt-ass naked I'll never know, but panic is a fickle thing. My only hope at that point, I realized, was to negotiate a path through the dining hall faster than Mardy could. My feet never quite made it all the way into my boots, but I refused to let that slow me down, as Mardy seemed hell-bent on claiming victory in our ongoing rivalry.

Naked, semi-booted, and gun in hand, I sprinted out of the bedroom. I heard a *whoomph* behind me as Mardy pushed her massive body through the wall. The entire structure shook with her weight as she began to charge behind me. Once out of the makeshift doorway that divides my room from the rest of the dining hall, I had a choice to turn left and try to outrun Mardy in a thirty-foot dash straight to the dining hall's front door or turn right and up the set of five stairs that connects the dining hall to the Atco trailer/camp kitchen behind.

Instinctively I turned right, hoping Mardy would have a hard time navigating the stairs. At the same time, I knew there was an exterior door at the far end of the kitchen trailer that opened to a fairly steep set of steel-grated stairs that led down to the ground below. Two sets of stairs—hopefully enough of an obstacle to slow a bear down and buy me some time. I figured that if I could make it through the kitchen and out the back door alive, I might have enough time to close the door and lock her inside. Failing that, maybe I could turn around and get a shot off in Mardy's direction.

Mardy was right behind me as I burst through the back door of the kitchen and into the cool of the night, my half-on/half-off boots scuffing under me as I sprinted. It wasn't easy to run, but the several hundred pounds of animal fury chasing me had kicked me into flight-or-fight mode, and I barely noticed as I leapt down the stairs to the ground and into the night air. I had no time to close the door behind me and she was too close for me get a shot off, so all I could do was run. To stop or stumble meant I was dead.

I knew it was also impossible to outrun her over any distance, so my only hope of escape was to get inside a more permanent structure or up and out of her reach. Then I spotted my salvation about twenty yards ahead, a steel ladder bolted to the end of one of the bunkhouses, which led to a spot on top I called The Perch, where I often went to look out over the horizon. With Mardy closing in, I threw my rifle up onto The Perch and then hit the ladder at full speed. As I started to scramble up, the bear took one final desperate swipe at me. Her claws sank into the rubber of my boots but mercifully landed in the empty space between the sole and my foot, which (thankfully) still hadn't made it to the bottom of the boot.

For an instant, time stood still as Mardy yanked onto my boot and I hung on to the ladder for dear life. Finally the boot gave way and the bear stumbled backward, long enough for me to finish the climb. Without thinking, I grabbed the rifle and hastily fired several shots through the twilight in Mardy's direction. The bear roared in return, a bone-chilling combination of anger and defiance as she took off toward the river and into the darkness.

Meanwhile, the commotion had roused my guests from their bunkhouses, and the hunters began to emerge onto the steel-grated landings outside their doors. Eventually, everyone was looking up toward me, the naked, one-booted lady with the rifle standing on the roof.

"Oh my god!" one of them screamed. "Are you OK?"

"I'm great!" I yelled down, trying my best to cover myself. "I've almost been eaten by a bear and all I'm wearing is a single boot! Looks like it's a photo op, boys…take advantage!"

Mardy was now well across the river and disappearing into willows and scrub brush on the other side. After covering myself with a blanket one of the hunters had tossed up, I climbed down and searched the area for blood. There was some, but not enough to indicate a direct hit. If I got her, it must have been a glancing blow at best. But as I continued to search the gravel, I came upon the single piece of damning evidence that confirmed her identity: lying on the gravel, blood still oozing out of it, was her ear…the identification tag still attached. I've kept that son of a bitch in a frame ever since.

After the near miss with Mardy, I doubled down on my efforts to make Kavik as bear-safe as possible. Given the camp's history, I knew nothing could make it 100 percent bear-*proof*, but I was going to do everything I could to protect myself and my guests in the meantime. I began by installing a series of floodlights around camp, which I could turn on with a single switch inside the dining hall. Most wild animals tend to be wary of artificial lighting, particularly when they associate it with things like badass gun-toting women. Even if they still decided to visit camp, at least I wouldn't be stumbling around in the dark trying to find them.

Some of my other safety measures were more rudimentary. To begin with, I had guns. A lot of guns. In fact, I owned so many rifles, shotguns, and handguns at one point that you could find them in almost every building in camp, except for the guests' accommodations. I also set up a series of noise traps around the camp, a rudimentary advance warning system that would hopefully give me a heads-up anytime a bear wandered too close. There was nothing sophisticated about the half-filled cans of gravel I peppered around the most important buildings, but at least the noise they created when they got knocked over would give me enough time to get my hands on a rifle before the next animal decided to make a meal of me. As a last resort, I even placed baseball bats in strategic locations around Kavik. If all else failed—or so the theory went—I'd grab some ash and swing for the fences.

While my bear-deterrent efforts bore fruit for a while, the one thing at Kavik that I could not control was the weather. I had spent a significant part of my life in Alaska and had grown comfortable with the rhythms and fury of winter, but Kavik was a different animal altogether. As the years passed, though, I became adept at anticipating changes in the weather. In that time, I learned that if you listen closely enough, the animals will tell you everything you need to know.

And on an evening the following February something was most definitely off. The larger animals were suddenly nowhere to be found; the smaller ones had gone into hiding in the space under the wooden floorboards of the dining hall and the ground below. There was an eerie stillness around Kavik, and I didn't like it one bit.

I went outside to try to figure out what was happening, though the profound dark of the winter night offered few clues in return. Until I looked straight up, that is, and saw something I'd never seen before: Shining dully overhead in a sky glazed with ice fog was the moon. And right beside it was *another* moon. I ran inside the dining hall and called my buddy Leroy, who worked for the National Weather Service down in Fairbanks.

"Dude, what the hell is going on?" I shouted through the crackling line. "I'm looking outside, and I see *two* moons!"

"Sue, is that you?" he called back. "Sue, listen to me. You need to batten down the hatches. You need to secure everything that you can, and you gotta do it *now*."

"Wait… Why?" I asked.

"It's a rare phenomenon called a 'mock moon' that only occurs when the winds aloft are so strong that they shift the ice crystals in the air," he said. "The second moon you're seeing is a refraction. But it means you're going to get hit with the mother of all storms. Get everything battened down now because you're gonna run out of time real soon."

Motivated equally by the uniqueness of a situation I'd never experienced and the urgency in Leroy's voice, I dashed around camp, frantically trying to secure as much as I could against what was coming. It was unbelievably cold to begin with—somewhere around –50°F—and the wind was going to take that down even lower before the night was out.

Then, without warning, what seemed like a giant airborne sinkhole opened up in the sky overhead and a blast of icy wind blew straight down to the ground below. In the years since, I've experienced several more of these "microbursts" or "downbursts," but on that February evening it scared the living shit out of me. The downdraft hit the ground like a bomb and then exploded in all directions. In an instant, everything in camp was compressed from above and then blown out sideways.

The steel ribs of the dining hall—each tube measuring more than fifty feet long and two inches thick—were bent downward with the force of the blast; the entire tent sagged dangerously under the pressure, and then *bam!* the bottom section of the dining hall ripped open completely. All around me, buildings compressed and debris flew wildly through the air.

Immediately after, a wind came from the east with enough force that it knocked me off my feet, followed by a wall of snow like a white tidal wave. I struggled to my feet and battled back to the dining hall, where I used some wood scraps and four-inch screws to patch it together as best I could before grabbing my jacket, gloves, and a flashlight and heading out into the maelstrom. It was so cold and the wind so strong I could barely breathe, but I knew that the survival of the camp rested on my shoulders alone. And there was no way in hell I was going down without a fight.

Over the howling of the wind, I heard strange noises coming from the gen shed some fifty yards behind me. Something had happened to the generator with the downburst, which was a massive problem because if the generator went out, all the power went with it. The sickly noise from the shed got progressively louder; then the generator quit completely and everything went black.

I made it about twenty feet before the wind and the cold became too much to bear. My hands had lost all feeling, and my face was frozen. Each breath was a stab wound to the chest. Suddenly I had become very small and very vulnerable in the face of such fury, so I turned tail and went back to the dining hall to wait out the storm.

It wasn't until the middle of the night that the wind began to die down to more manageable levels. I didn't have the luxury of sleep, so I bundled up and went outside again. It was still snowing like hell, but at least I could navigate my way around camp somewhat through the knee-high drifts that were growing bigger with each passing hour. My first stop was the small wooden building that houses Kavik's water tanks, its door now partially torn from its frame. I propped the door back in position and then tried to screw a scrap of wood across its face to seal it and stop more snow from blowing in.

I fumbled with the screws in my gloved hands, but it was nearly impossible to do anything in the cold. I don't know what the windchill was, but at minus fifty degrees and with a constant wind of about twenty miles per hour, it felt close to –90°F. I managed to hold the screw in my hand and start the drill; luckily the battery didn't die until after the screw took hold in the wood. Then I started making my way back to the gen shed. Meanwhile, the blowing snow had found its way into each opening the blizzard had carved into Kavik's many buildings.

I made it back to the gen shed where massive drifts were forming inside the twenty-foot-high building, but the weather was still too bad for me to do anything other than assess the damage. If my headlamp or flashlight quit unexpectedly in the midst of the storm, I might never find my way back to the safety of the dining hall. So all I could do was hope that the storm would let up and leave me something to salvage.

Eventually the storm broke, but the damage the blizzard left in its wake was on a scale I'd never seen before. Everywhere I looked, pieces of buildings had been torn off, equipment scattered, some damaged beyond repair. The twin outhouses at the back of camp near The Boneyard had blown away completely. I spent most of my efforts trying to reclaim the gen shed, the biggest building in camp at almost twenty-five feet tall and forty feet wide. The two wooden doors that sealed its entrance—each eight feet across and almost fifteen feet tall—had been ripped off their hinges and were lying on top of the machinery inside. Inside, the snow drifts were ten feet tall in places.

It would take me the better part of a week to dig out the gen shed, first by hand and later with the Bobcat I eventually unearthed inside, a week of no power and not much natural light. Thankfully the heaters never quit, so I was able to warm myself when the cold became overwhelming. As for collecting the pieces of camp that the storm had blown around—the wall of an outhouse here, a door there—it would take months to complete, and it wasn't until the summer when all the snow had melted that I finally recovered the flotsam and jetsam of my life.

Yet through it all, I never considered the prospect of giving up and moving on. There were much "easier" lifestyles on Earth—I had lived some of them—but in the long run, they never appealed to my sensibilities. If anything, the storm, Mardy, and the foxes had shown me that if I, indeed, had a place in the world, it was there. I had survived on sheer grit, a finite stash of supplies, and the knowledge that nobody was coming to save me. It was just me and the land, and yet, as brutal as it was, I felt alive in a way I never could in "civilization."

There's a purity to this place that no city or town can ever match. The silence that settled after the storm was deafening, an emptiness that wasn't empty at all but full of life waiting to resume. The air was raw and honest, each breath a reminder that I was part of something vast and untamed. Deep down, I had come know one absolute: The wilderness doesn't ask for pretense or masks; it demands only truth. My truth was simple: Kavik was where I belonged.

I wasn't prepared for what came next, though.

CHAPTER 7

LEFT FOR DEAD

2008. The last of my guests had left in mid-September and I had already been alone for a few weeks, slowly settling back into the rhythm of another winter on my own at Kavik. I knew from experience that other than the occasional pilot stopping in for fuel, I likely wouldn't see another human for months to come. Like they always had, those months would test the limits of my endurance and resolve. At the same time, though, I was buffeted by the profound contentment that came with living my life exactly as I was meant to. No schedule, no boss, no phone calls, no deadlines. Just me and the snow-clad hills that rolled endlessly away in any direction until they hit the mountains or the sea.

But when you call the wilderness home, you're never truly alone, no matter how far away the nearest human may reside. I had the foxes; they had become near-constant companions in and around camp, and I derived strength from their furtive company, which offered a sense of connection to the world around me. I observed their resourcefulness and resilience every day, and they gave me strength in the most challenging circumstances, offered beauty and joy in the thousands of small moments we shared together.

Far more troubling than the foxes were the bears. Despite my many attempts at making the camp less appealing, the grizzlies had been frequenting Kavik more often as summer wound to a close, and I knew few things would make them happier than feasting on a juicy hunk of flesh like me before denning for the winter. Since their survival is dependent on accumulating enough fat reserves to make it through the lean months to come, Alaskan grizzly bears need to eat furiously before hibernating. This period of intense feeding, called hyperphagia, sees bears consume up to twenty thousand calories per day in anticipation of what lies ahead.

Typically Alaskan grizzlies dine on things like salmon (when they can get it), berries, roots and plants, small mammals, and whatever carrion they come across on the tundra, but that didn't mean they would pass up an opportunity to add a whole lotta woman-meat to their bellies if they had the chance. I've never known exactly where I stand on the food chain, but it has always been clear that at Kavik, the top spot is the exclusive preserve of the grizz. Sure, I had my guns, but with the bear activity having reached a fevered pitch in the preceding weeks, guns alone might not be enough to save me from an animal motivated to take me down.

By late October, the snow had already started to settle in for the winter, peppering the hills around Kavik with the beginnings of a white blanket that would persist until May or June, when brown patches of grass would begin to peek through and herald the coming of summer. That was a long way off, though, and for now temperatures had already dipped below zero, the days much shorter than they had been just a few weeks before.

By that time, the bears had largely finished their voracious food consumption, had scouted their denning sites, and were preparing to hibernate. Their visits to camp had slowly become less regular, as grizzlies on the verge of hibernation don't range as far as they do in the summer, instead choosing to stay close to the den to hunt or feed. And once the temperature started dipping below zero consistently, I knew they'd soon bed down until spring.

Comfortable in the knowledge that I had made it through another summer without a dangerous encounter, I was taken by complete surprise when a new grizzly moved into the area near Kavik. I first spotted him wandering the hills across the river to the west of camp, a young male likely between four and seven years old and tipping the scales at approximately five hundred pounds. But more than his unexpected appearance in my backyard, what struck me as odd about this bear was his behavior. Instead of preparing to bed down, the young grizz seemed more interested in carving out his place among the older, more established creatures in the area... including me.

I call these kinds of up-and-coming bears *betas*, the ones that want to climb to the top of the social ladder and become alphas, which is the only way to ensure their chance at mating regularly. (Animal biologists don't typically use such terms as "alpha" and "beta"—which tend to be reserved for wolves and other pack animals—to describe the social structure of grizzly bears, but I've always found them perfect for describing how individual bears assert dominance over others in such situations as mating and feeding.) And in the bear world, female grizzlies make a habit of mating with alphas, not betas.

Becoming an alpha is no easy task, though, and begins with a beta first making himself known to the other bears in the area. In the social dynamics of grizzly bears, dominance and hierarchy are everything, and although grizzly bears are typically solitary, betas will go out of their way to engage in otherwise uncharacteristic behaviors to challenge and/or replace an alpha bear.

This behavior takes many forms and usually begins with such benign intimidation tactics as posturing and physical displays of strength such as standing tall on their hind legs, roaring, and making otherwise aggressive movements. If these don't prove effective, a beta might escalate his actions to direct physical confrontations. This often occurs when a beta challenges the alpha's strength by attempting to access resources, like food or even mates, in the alpha's presence. An alpha that acquiesces gives a signal of weakness, providing the beta an opportunity to claim dominance, and betas will *always* exploit signs of vulnerability in the alpha. From what I had seen, the journey from beta to alpha was complete when the less-dominant bear achieved two of three behavioral benchmarks: subjugate the alpha, take over the alpha's territory, or, in extreme cases, kill the alpha. I call it an "alpha push."

And back in mid-October 2008, the beta had apparently set his sights on Kavik and its alpha: me.

Things remained civil between the beta and me for a couple of weeks after his arrival, until the morning I went to check the levels in the aviation-fuel tanks on the north end of camp, where I found a caribou carcass half-buried in the gravel of my helicopter pad. I couldn't be sure, but I had a pretty good idea the beta was responsible. At that time of year, no other bear preparing for the lean months of hibernation to come was going to sacrifice a perfectly good carcass just to make a statement. The beta was making his alpha push, and if my years of observing bear behavior had taught me anything, it was that *I* was the next box to be checked off on his résumé: He was making a very clear statement that he intended to take over *my* territory.

This might be a problem, I thought. The bear apparently had no intention on settling down for the winter until Kavik was his. With absolutely no idea how to handle the rapidly developing situation, I called my friends the wildlife troopers in Fairbanks for advice.

"This is no joke, Sue," one of them said after hearing my tale. "This bear seems to be making a direct challenge to your authority, and I think it means business."

"I think so too," I said.

"In terms of safety, I'd say the best thing for you to do is either burn that caribou carcass or just haul it down to the river. The last thing you want is for that thing to start rotting on your doorstep. It'll attract every hungry bear for miles around. But whatever you decide, make sure you keep an eye out for that beta. And do *not* go outside without a gun."

"Well, burning it will use too much fuel, and I barely have enough to make it through the winter as it is," I said. "I'll bring it to the river."

I knew that removing the carcass would minimize the risk of bringing other bears into camp looking for a quick meal before they went to sleep. More important, though, was the fact that it would send a clear message to the beta: *This is my land; don't fuck with it.* Yet at the same time, something told me that I needed to do more if I truly wanted to send the bear away for good. I needed to show him that I was Kavik's alpha and had no intention of relinquishing that title.

So I didn't just dig up the carcass. At the helicopter pad, I stood over the dead caribou and raised myself up to as great a height as possible, like any badass alpha would have done in the same situation. I kicked away the snow and gravel in billowing clouds of gray-white smoke, tore up the gravel with a shovel, tossed it high in the air. I stamped and huffed and roared in as deep and frightening a voice as I could muster. Then, when the caribou was finally out of the ground and loaded into the back of the quad, I poured ammonia on the spot to mimic urine and mark my territory. (Bears use many different kinds of urine scents to communicate with each other, but urine heavy in ammonia is a challenge scent and usually means *find someplace else to play*.)

I guess I shouldn't have been particularly surprised to see the beta watching me from a grassy bar in the middle of the riverbed a couple hundred yards away, but what he did then scared the living shit out of me. The beta actually seemed to be mimicking me as he bellowed, roared, and used his powerful front paws to tear moss, brush, and boulders from the ground and toss it around. My exhibition of strength had done little to deter the beta. In fact, I may have just pissed him off.

Either way, there was still a dead caribou in the quad that I needed to get rid of. I hopped into the driver's seat and drove north along the runway that borders the eastern edge of camp until I reached the end, where a trail snakes through the willows to the steep bank perched some twenty feet above the Kavik River. Below me, the riverbed was almost a mile wide, its braided threads of water already beginning to freeze for the winter. I clicked off the safety of the .44 on my hip, took a long look around for the bear, and dragged the hundred-pound caribou carcass to the edge. Then I pushed it over.

It didn't take long for me to realize the beta had most assuredly *not* gotten the message. Over the next few days, I saw regular signs of him, only this time much closer to my home. Now his plate-sized paw prints crisscrossed the snow between the trailers directly in camp, sometimes only a few yards from where I slept inside the dining hall tent. It was like Mardy all over again. I was terrified at the notion of living through another experience like that, but life at Kavik didn't stop just because I was scared. My myriad daily responsibilities continued unabated, responsibilities that required constant attention, especially now that winter had begun to deepen, the sun carving a progressively lower arc across the sky with each passing day. And one of my most important jobs in that time of year was securing as much water as I could for the frozen months to come.

Although the main branch of the river had now completely iced over, I could still draw from the free-flowing water underneath, which would help me top up my water tanks one last time before the Kavik froze solid. To do so, I'd have to make one final visit to the river with a portable water pump, which I would then connect to a couple of flexible hundred-foot hoses that, in turn, I connected to the pipes that led back to the tanks in the water shed a few dozen yards behind the dining hall.

It was ten below outside. I put on two pairs of insulated Carhartt bib overalls and then made my way down to the river. The willows formed a four-foot-high wall of brush on either side of me as I walked down the trail, equipment in one hand, rifle in the other, .44 in my holster. The willows had shed their leaves weeks before with the change of weather, but there was still enough camouflage for the beta to hide himself. So I was extra careful as I made my way, stopping frequently to scan the surroundings for any movement.

With no sign of the bear anywhere, I set to the task at hand. The first order of business was to knock a hole in the ice layer covering the river with my ax, into which I'd drop the suction hose from the pump. What I didn't know at the time was that the bear was hiding behind me in a cutbank, a sheltered area at the bottom of a steep section of the river's bank. So although he was probably only about twenty yards from where I was standing, he was completely obscured from view. Meanwhile, I needed both hands to break the ice with the ax, so I set the rifle down and got to work. But shortly after my hands were empty of the gun and I had bent over the ice, the bear pounced.

My ears were filled with the crack of the ax hitting the ice and my own heavy breathing, I didn't hear the beta until it was too late. Before I even had a chance to connect my thoughts, the bear snatched me from the back like I was a salmon and began dragging me away.

Despite the gravity of the circumstances, I didn't panic. I had been around bears most of my life and knew a fair bit about their behavior. In that moment I figured I had a chance to live, since I knew the beta would likely be more interested in showing the other bears in the area what a badass he was by beating up on the alpha of Kavik than he was in killing me. And if he was, indeed, going to finish me, he was going to take his time doing it. That fact, I thought, might save my life. Ultimately, it did.

The bear dragged me across the river like a rag doll, up the bank, then onto the bumpy hummocks of the tundra to the west. I only had a second or two to contemplate my fate before he grabbed me with his paw and began batting me from side to side. I am not a small woman, but the bear seemed to exert little, if any, effort each time he smacked me and lifted me off the ground. I heard a sickening crunch as pain exploded from my hips and then cried out in agony as he threw me to the ground in a heap and wandered off. Seemingly spurred on by my cries, the bear returned and snatched me by the head with his mouth. He shook me violently that way and then snapped his jaws on my throat and began to apply pressure before mercifully dropping me to the turf once again.

I could feel blood running freely from the various lacerations and punctures in my body but didn't have more than a moment to take stock of my condition before the bear was on top of me again, this time slicing his claws through my thick jacket like it wasn't even there and then ripping them across my shoulder in a hot, flesh-melting tear of indescribable pain. I could barely breathe but desperately swallowed huge gulps of air in the seconds between attacks. Through it all, I never fought back because I knew that to do so would surely ensure my death. There are varying schools of thought on this, but from what I'd seen, grizzly bears only get more pissed off when their prey fights back, and the last thing I wanted the beta to think was that I was ready to rumble.

Once again, the bear released me from his grasp and I tumbled to the ground in a heap of pain and adrenaline. Time stood still. The bear had been playing with me for about ten minutes now, and I knew he would soon decide to either kill me or simply move on. And all I could do was lie there and await my fate.

Luckily, the bear seemed to opt for the latter option. Looking back, I can only attribute his actions to the fact that he was not yet an alpha. Alone at the top of the complex hierarchy that defines bear relationships, an alpha grizzly answers only to itself. It eats when it wants, mates when it wants, and kills when it wants. A beta has to fight for that respect, so when it kills something, it needs to make sure the other animals in the area know exactly what it's doing.

With that, the bear resumed his attack on me, dragging me another fifty yards across the tundra where he lifted me and battered me onto the frozen hummocks below, my legs bent at sickening angles behind and under me. Then he lumbered off toward the riverbank where he stopped and roared, a bone-chilling sound that echoed to the hills in the distance as he began ripping bushes from the ground, bellowing all the while.

Unable to move, I lay still and watched as the bear made a series of bluff charges at me. He galloped across the tundra with frightening speed, muscles rippling with each stride, to the spot where he had deposited me a few moments before. Each time he reached me, he batted me around with his massive forepaws; each time I felt his thick claws sink into my body. Each time I waited for death to come.

But the bear was in no mood to end me that quickly. Back and forth, back and forth we went. Each time he returned he smacked me, mauled me, tossed me, roared. Once again, he wrapped his massive jaws around my throat and I waited for the inevitable, but the bear stopped once again and loped off, tearing up the brush and bellowing all the way.

On the last charge, the beta put his jaws around my head and started to squeeze. To this day I can smell his thick, musty breath as it washed over my face and I heard the sound of my skull cracking in his teeth. It's a sound I hope nobody else ever has to hear. Because no matter how tough you think you are, nothing on Earth can prepare you for the sound of your own skull cracking in the jaws of a grizzly.

So this is how I die, I thought. I didn't have much time to contemplate the relative merits of my life in that moment because I was primarily focused on a level of pain I didn't even know existed. But I remember having a moment of clarity as the bear clamped down on my skull. If that was going to be my end, I was OK with it. I'd had a good run and had lived most of my life on my own terms, surrounded by the beauty I'd chosen to be my personal backdrop. I'd been the best mother and wife that I could. I was ready to die.

But the inevitable never came. Rather than kill me, the bear dragged me back toward the river, knocked me over the bank to the rocks and ice below, and ran off to the west, still bellowing and roaring as he did. Only this time, he didn't stop right away. I couldn't see the beta from the riverbed, but I could hear his cries recede into the distance. But even as they got progressively quieter and moved farther away, the sound was terrifying: 100 percent pure animal testosterone.

At that moment, I realized the bear had given me an unintended chance at survival. Odds were that he'd soon come back to finish the job, but with him having ventured farther afield this time, I figured this was my only opportunity to make it back to the relative safety of camp. And if not, at least I'd die trying.

I took stock of my condition. I was sticky with my own blood, which was dripping from the innumerable wounds that tattooed my body. My hips had been torn from their sockets, and I couldn't see clearly through the snow, grit, and blood that obscured my vision. My skull was punctured, and something felt horribly wrong with my spine. And yet I had one clear thought: *Get to camp. No matter what you do, get your ass back to camp.*

My rifle lay downriver, the .44 had been ripped from its holster and was scattered somewhere on the tundra, and I had no intention of going back for either of them. Camp lay ahead, the bear had dragged me one step closer to salvation, and I wasn't going to ruin the opportunity by going returning for my weapons. I figured my window of opportunity was incredibly small. Bears are terrifyingly fast when they want to be, and if the beta caught sight of me, I was as good as dead.

Slowly I got to my feet as the world swam before my eyes. I lost my balance, stumbled, fell hard on the ice, and then pulled myself up again, determined to stay upright this time no matter what. My legs sticking out at unholy angles, I limped and stumbled across the river, up the bank on the other side and across the uneven, snow-covered turf toward camp, only sixty yards away. It wasn't much distance to cover, but for the walking dead on the North Slope of Alaska, it felt like a hundred miles. One fucking step at a time… just one, then another…rinse and repeat. Never looking back, I shuffled toward salvation.

By some act of mercy, I made it to the dining hall and closed the door behind me. I didn't know how long I'd be able to stay conscious, so the first thing I did was grab the air-to-ground radio.

"This is Sue from Kavik," I called into the receiver. "I've been attacked by a grizzly and need some assistance." The response—from someone working at an oil field up in Prudhoe Bay—was not what I expected to hear.

"Hey, I'm sorry but this is a secure channel," a man's voice gruffly replied. Then nothing.

"Hello?" I cried into the receiver. "*Hello?*" No reply.

I grabbed the analog phone and called my trooper buddies in Fairbanks. When the call went to voicemail, I left a message explaining that I'd had a run-in with a bear and needed help. (The troopers would later tell me that my message sounded so calm that they didn't realize I was hurt. They just thought there had been another encounter with the beta we had spoken about a few weeks earlier.)

I was on my own.

If I was going to survive, my first priority was to address the physical damage and take care of my injuries as best I could. I knew that bears have bacteria in their saliva that can cause latent infections for years. So I scrubbed the wounds on my head, shoulders, and hips with betadine and soap before flushing them all with alcohol, a process that helped me discover swear words I didn't even know existed.

After washing my wounds, I pulled out my suture kit and began to stitch up the most egregious ones: first the shoulder, then the head, then everything else I could get my hands on. It wasn't the neatest work, hurt like absolute fucking hell, and was nearly impossible to do on my own body, but I needed to stop the bleeding as best I could. As for my dislocated hips, I had little choice but to try to get them back in place, which I did by lying on my back on a table, letting my legs dangle off the edge, then pushing each one down and away from my body in a slow, deliberate motion (more new swear words). Then I tightened my gun belt around my hips, hoping against hope it would keep them in place long enough for me to finish the job. Shock began to stir at the edges of my sanity, and I knew I had to keep moving because there was one more job to do: face the bear.

The beta had just served me with my eviction notice, and I knew that if I wasn't gone when he returned to camp, nothing would stop him from finishing me off. The choice was clear: One of us had to die, and I wasn't ready to meet my maker. *I* was Kavik's alpha, and like any alpha, I wasn't gonna let any beta take it from me without a fight.

It was hardly an easy decision, though. I was in excruciating pain and had just survived the most horrific thing I had ever experienced in my life. On the one hand, I just wanted to curl up in a ball on my bed, cover myself with a blanket, and wish it all away. I was more scared than I'd ever been, and the residual terror I felt coursed through my veins like a drug. Would the bear be hiding in wait again? Would I even have the strength to pull the trigger if I got him in my sights?

At the same time, though, another, stronger feeling began to well up inside me: rage. I knew the bear was just acting on instinct, but I fumed at the thought of what it had done to me. Deep down, I knew I would never be the same. What's more, I knew the bear would always be a threat to my existence. If the beta lived, I could never take another step in or around camp without wondering if he was hiding behind the next corner. I could not—and would not—live my life in that kind of fear.

Burning with a desire to regain control of my now-precarious existence, I took one last look around the dining hall, knowing full well it might be the last time I ever did so. Then I walked outside, fueled by a raw and singular determination. Every sound was magnified, every shadow a beacon of light as I took my first determined steps outside to face my fate, to live or die.

It was time for Kavik's last stand.

CHAPTER 8

KAVIK'S LAST STAND

Adrenaline is a wondrous thing. The same force that lets mothers lift cars off trapped children, it turns agony into background noise, fear into fuel, and impossibility into instinct. My body was torn and broken, but it didn't matter...the drug coursing through my veins numbed the pain. I moved on pure drive, each step a defiance of biology. In that moment, I wasn't just a survivor, I was the storm rolling back out into the wild.

Still, I opened the door to the dining hall warily, unsure if the beta had wandered back into Kavik after the attack. Under normal circumstances, I pride myself on knowing everything that's going on in and around camp, but I was too focused on tending my wounds to know what the bear had been doing while I was in the dining hall. There was a very good chance he'd followed me and was nearby, waiting for another opportunity to pounce on me unawares. But I was anything but unaware. As I stepped out onto the snow and took my first few unsteady steps across the ground, I felt more alive and aware than I had perhaps ever been in my life.

The cold bit through my clothes, sharpening my senses to a razor's edge. I looked around at a landscape I'd come to know like the back of my hand. Kavik was my home, but in that moment it felt vast and indifferent, the snow-covered expanse on every side echoing my isolation. My heart was racing, but I tried to calm my breathing because I knew I'd have to be steady when the time came to pull the trigger. I listened intently for sounds of the beta as I walked through camp, whipping around every corner with my handgun held out in front of me like a cop in a movie. My breath hung in the air like a ghostly mist as the adrenaline pumped mercilessly through my veins. Every sound was magnified, every reflection on the snow a beacon of light. After a few minutes, I realized the bear had not followed me back to camp after all, so I decided to head back out to the tundra to meet him on his own turf.

I walked toward the northern edge of camp, where the trail descends through the willows and down toward the river. Fear churned in my gut as my mind raced with images of the beta—its hulking frame bashing me from side to side with frightening ease, the glint of its teeth as it clamped down on my skull, the brutal matter-of-factness of the attack. At the same time, my fear was mingled with anger, a hot rage that grew with every step. It was no longer just about the beta; it was about reclaiming control over my own life in a place where nature's hierarchy is law. I had always been comfortable with the predator–prey relationship, but this had evolved into something even more primal: kill or be killed.

I spotted him as I slowly descended the trail toward the river. The beta had continued to move west across the tundra away from camp and was now about a mile off, pacing and making the same sort of ruckus he did when he was mauling me. Immediately I knew this was my opportunity: By making so much of a fuss, the bear might not notice me creeping along the tundra as I approached. With any luck, he would be as deaf to my movements as I was to his back when I was chipping a hole in the river. Had it only been twenty minutes since I crawled back? It seemed like an eternity.

A cold breeze blew across my face as I crept; the wind was in my favor. Slowly, cautiously, and unsteadily, I limped down to the riverbed, where I inched my way across its icy, boulder-strewn surface. I figured I was relatively safe down there, obscured from the bear's vision and with the wind blowing toward me. All I had to do was get up the opposite bank and hope he wasn't waiting for me when I did.

One fucking step at a time.

I got to the other side and scrambled warily up the fifteen feet that separated the riverbed from the wide expanse of tundra above. As I neared the top and came into full view, I dropped onto all fours and crawled, elbow over elbow, knee over knee, with my handgun held religiously in front of me the whole time. As I did, doubt crept into my brain. *What if you fail?* it asked me. *What if this is the last mistake you make?*

The thoughts threatened to stopped me dead in my tracks. But I shoved them aside and instead tried to focus on everything that had brought me to that moment in time: my willpower, my resourcefulness, my bull-headed refusal to yield in the most challenging circumstances. Never in my life had I given in to the voices of doubt, and I had no intention of starting then. If I didn't face the bear, I'd never sleep another peaceful night at Kavik.

As I crested the far side of the bank, I breathed a sigh of relief: The bear still seemed unaware of my presence. I edged the thoughts of pain out of my consciousness and focused on the task at hand, crouching and crawling ever closer to the beta. The snow crunched faintly beneath my body, but the steady breeze in my face masked my sounds. I edged ever closer, making sure not to crack the thinly frozen pools of water that peppered the tundra. To break through one would give away my location…and my advantage.

I got to within two hundred yards, my eyes locked on the bear. His fur rippled in the faint light; his muscles shifted with every movement; his ears twitched instinctively as he scanned the landscape for the sounds of opportunity or danger. Thankfully, the beta seemed more intent on rooting through the ground than worrying about anything approaching, including me. The smell of musk and raw earth drifted faintly on the breeze, mingling with the metallic tang of blood in my mouth, a remnant from some yet-untended wound.

Slowly and cautiously, I slid the rifle off my shoulder, my heart now pounding uncontrollably in my chest as I tried to calm my breathing. If ever my aim needed to be true, that was the moment. If I wounded the beta, he would undoubtedly fly into a rage and attack his attacker with a fury even I couldn't imagine. Grizzly bears are incredibly resilient, with thick hides, dense muscle, and a reinforced skull that can deflect a poorly aimed shot from even the most powerful rifle. If I was going to win the battle, my first shot needed to hit the beta directly in its vital organs or the brain. I may not have a chance to pull the trigger twice.

I lifted the rifle to my shoulder and looked through the scope. A gust of wind briefly changed direction, and I froze as the bear's head snapped up and he tested the air. My heart stopped as I waited for his imminent charge; if he started running I'd have to shoot him right between the eyes to stop him, which would be nearly impossible. Mercifully, he didn't catch sight of me and turned sideways again, offering me a perfect view of his entire, impressive length. I picked a spot just behind his front shoulders, the gateway to his vital organs inside. The moment of truth had arrived, a culmination of everything I'd gone through in the past hour. My fingers tightened around the weapon, survival against annihilation.

I inhaled slowly and held my breath as I squeezed the trigger.

The roar of the rifle echoed across the frozen expanse, deafening in the stillness. For a moment, time seemed to stop, and then the beta collapsed to the ground in a heap. My shot was true and had hit him right in his vital area, and I was pretty sure it was a one-shot kill. But I wasn't taking any chances with an animal that only a few minutes before was hell-bent on my destruction. Two more times I shot, two more times I struck him in his vital area. Then I stopped and watched. I waited to see if the bear moved, watched for a steam of breath, but it never came. After a few minutes I started hobbling to the spot where the beta had fallen. As I drew close, I marveled at his sheer size and power, both even more imposing up close. Here was an animal as beautiful as it was terrifying, a creature built to survive and thrive in the harshest of worlds.

When I reached the spot where the bear lay, I poked it with my rifle a few times to make sure there was no sign of life. Then I looked around, scanning the landscape for any other predators that might have been drawn by the sound of the shot. The wilderness felt eerily quiet, the wind carrying only its cold, unrelenting bite. Secure in the knowledge that the bear was really gone, I collapsed on the ground, laid my head on his still-warm body, and wept.

Relief washed over me as the tears poured out. The immediate danger was over, the beta now still and silent underneath me. At the same time, though, an overwhelming, visceral wave of raw emotion welled up inside me: triumph, loss, guilt, sadness, and exhaustion.

Despite everything that the beta had done to me, despite the dislocations and the broken bones, the mangled spine, the lacerations and punctures that would scar my body for the rest of my life, I felt sad at having taken his life. Even in self-defense, the weight of having killed was not lost on me.

In the minutes that followed, those emotions began to be replaced by things far more pressing and visceral, though. One by one, like a row of dominoes, my feelings were knocked down by a thing so massive and all-consuming that it threatened to drop me on the spot: pain. It clawed at every level of my being, left no part of my body untouched. From the crown of my head to the soles of my feet, my reality became brutally simple: I was in immense, intense, raging, nauseating, screaming, crippling pain.

With the adrenaline that had once raged through my veins now slowing to a crawl, I knew it wouldn't be long before I was struck down by the enormity of what the beta had done to my body. Suddenly, getting back to camp became the sole purpose of my existence. But before doing so, I had one last tribute to make. I reached into my pocket, pulled out one of the heart-shaped stones I kept there for good luck, and placed it on the bear. Then, as I stood and turned back toward the river and camp beyond, a strange calm settled over me. The chaos of the encounter faded, replaced by a grim sense of accomplishment. I was alive. Against all odds, I had survived.

Slowly I began to hobble back toward Kavik, inch by inch.

Eventually I made it to the western bank of the river, collapsed onto my rear end and slid down the trail to the rocky, icy bed below where I began to shuffle my way across. The pain increased with every step, eventually reaching a level I'd never before experienced.

I tried to will it away, but the tears rolled uncontrollably down my face and the world began to swim once again. Then, when I was about halfway across the river, my dislocated hips finally gave out and I collapsed with a scream that nobody could hear. This time, though, no belt was going to hold them in place. Lying on my stomach on the icy river, I started dragging myself toward the safety of the dining hall. Despite the effort, I kept the rifle draped over my left shoulder, no matter how much it slowed me down. No ghost bear was going to swallow me.

With each foot of river that I dragged myself over, I moaned audibly. I was close to losing consciousness, the world around me blurry, spinning. I wanted to stop and rest, perhaps even sleep for a while, but at the same time I know that doing so would likely ensure my death. The bear was dead, but a lot of other critters would love to claim my unconscious body, including perhaps the deadliest foe of all—the temperature. So I kept dragging myself toward camp, arm over arm, one painful patch of ground at a time disappearing behind me.

After what seemed like an eternity, I made it back to the east bank of the river, where I clawed my way up the trail through the willows and to the gravel of camp. Finally, I pulled myself through the entryway of the dining hall and into the warmth of the room. With what little remaining energy I had, I stood up and swept my arm along the entire length of the shelf where I kept a variety of chips and candy bars for guests to munch on as they pleased; they fell to the ground in a heap. Then I yanked a case of bottled water onto the wooden floor, the last vestige of strength I had as my body finally gave out and I collapsed in a heap amid the chips and chocolate bars and water bottles that would sustain me until I recovered, help arrived, or I died.

Unlike the first time I returned after the attack, I could no longer reach the air-to-ground radio or the analog phone, both of which were perched on a shelf high on the wall. In fact, I couldn't move at all. Then I blacked out.

To this day I don't know how long I lay there unconscious. Eventually I opened my eyes, only to realize that my legs and shoulders had completely seized up. I couldn't move other than to lean to the left or right to grab some food or drink; I had absolutely no way to reach the outside world. At first, I refused to accept my fate. I had survived the attack, had stalked and killed the bear that threatened my life, had crawled back to camp like an animal. This was *not* how I was going to die. Plus, both the air-to-ground radio and the phone were *right there*, not more than fifteen feet from where I lay. Surely I could get up and grab one of them.

I tried. Again and again and again I tried. And again and again and again I crumpled to the ground before I even made it to my knees. I had maybe a dozen snack-size bags of chips, a handful of candy bars, and a case of water bottles to survive on until help arrived in the spring. Reality felt like a distant nightmare, but it was all too real, and it was mine.

Despite the gravity of my situation, I sprang into full-blown survival mode immediately after I regained consciousness. I made endless calculations in my head. *How long can I make the chips and candy last? How much water should I ration? How do I stay warm if the heater fails? And how on Earth do I tell the outside world I'm here and need help?*

I counted and then recounted my supplies, trying to convince myself I had enough. The fear of starvation gnawed at the edges of my thoughts, but I pushed it aside. The days that followed were a blur of agony, shame, and anger. Day blended into night; consciousness waxed and waned. Thirsty. Drink a little water. Not too much; it has to last. Hungry. Only chips and Snickers. Thank goodness I got some Cheetos. *Maybe there's a god after all!* I laughed.

Though they had slowed to a crawl, my bodily functions didn't stop, and I still couldn't move. So whatever I had to do, I did it right there. Between the pain and the fear and the hunger and the sadness, that indignity was likely the worst part of all.

Lying there in silence, the sounds of life outside the tent became more acute than usual: the foxes scurrying through camp;

the telltale *swoosh* of a raven's feathers as it flew by; wind blowing snow across the tent. Meanwhile, my body ached in places and in ways I'd never before imagined. Even the slightest shift was excruciating. Panic threatened to take hold, but I clung to the hope that my strength would return. *It has to*, I thought.

By the third or fourth day after I regained consciousness, I began to sink into a deep, hollow exhaustion. Hunger clawed at my stomach, but I stuck to my rationing plan, eating only a few chips a day and drinking no more than half of a small bottle of water. My mind began to spiral. *What if this is how it ends?* I'd survived so much in my life; the thought of it ending there on the floor of the dining hall in my own waste was almost too much to bear.

I spun through the memories like records on an old turntable. The stark realization that my mother wasn't coming back for me. Meeting Eddie for the first time. Giving birth to Jennie and Jesse. Joe and Jack and the biological father I'd never know. I passed the hours by replaying conversations, arguments, and moments of joy and ached for a world I would likely never return to. With nothing else to do, I began to reflect on the life I'd led, the choices I'd made, the myriad little moments I'd taken for granted along the way. I had regrets, sure, but I had also tried to live an honest, decent life. It wasn't always pretty, but I could look back on it knowing that I'd usually been motivated by good. And even then, as I sunk to the depths of despair, I was encouraged by the small embers of resolve that refused to burn out inside my soul. *I'm still alive*, I reminded myself, over and over, like a mantra.

On the fifth day after I regained consciousness (I kept count by scratching tally marks into the wooden floor), the noises of the vast Alaskan wilderness were interrupted by a man-made sound when a plane flew high overhead, punctuated by chatter on the air-to-ground radio. It was my salvation, my chance to let someone know I was here. I tried with every fiber of my being to stand up and walk the few yards that separated me from the radio, but my body simply would not respond. I tried to roll over onto all fours and crawl but didn't have the strength. I was frozen in time and space, a mummy slowly wasting away to a slow, undignified death as I wallowed there in my own shit.

Eventually, someone seemed to notice they hadn't heard from me in a while. Most of my winters at Kavik were spent alone, but the community of "remote people," as we call ourselves, is a tight one nonetheless. Like in the rest of Alaska, residents of even the most far-flung places look out for one another, likely because we all understand the stakes when things go sideways. And of all the people who watch out for one another, perhaps none are more important than the bush pilots, our eyes and ears in the skies. Whether the product of their own boredom or a deep sense of responsibility, bush pilots *always* used the radio to call down to camp when they were passing overhead. Like Mukluk Messaging, it was a way to share news of the area and check in on people who live on the razor's edge of survival.

On the morning of my seventh day on the floor, the

air-to-ground crackled to life once more. This time, though, the message was directed at me from a bush pilot named Ben, whom I'd known for years.

"*Sue? Sue...you there?*" he said. "*I see your Bobcat over by the fuel shed and your pump in the river. Guess you must be out and about working. All right, I'll try you again soon.*" Then the radio went silent.

I screamed as loud as I could, pounded my hands on the wooden floor. But even as I did, the sound of the plane got progressively quieter. It was excruciating. My salvation was *right there* on the wall, not far from where I lay on the floor, but I was physically incapable of moving that far, even to save my own life.

On day 8, with my water supply nearly drained and the chips and chocolate bars all but gone, I heard another bush plane pass low overhead. Once again, its presence was accompanied by a call on the radio that I simply could not answer. This time it was Jim, a pilot from Fairbanks who often made trips to the Prudhoe Bay to supply the oil camps up there with people, fuel, and other supplies.

"*Sue? I guess it's pretty foggy down there. I can't see much, but I hope you're OK. You must be out doing stuff. Don't need any fuel this time but will see you again sometime.*"

The emotional letdown that accompanied Jim's call was monumental, his voice like a nightmare I couldn't wake up from. My body felt like a shell—hollow, weak, barely functional. Even the smallest movement, whether to pick up a chip, nibble the stub of a KitKat, or take a tiny sip of my rapidly disappearing water, was a herculean effort, a battle against the mounting lethargy inside. For the first time since the beta started to squeeze my skull in his jaws, I seriously began to consider that death was imminent. In retrospect, it would have made a much cooler story to die in the bear's mouth. At least there was an adventure in that. Lying in your own shit on the floor on the dining hall? Not so much. But I resolved to face my end with dignity nonetheless. As I filtered in and out of consciousness, I felt a profound gratitude. Gratitude for the first time I set eyes on the little ramshackle cabin at the end of the Chena road. Gratitude for the children I'd brought into the world. Gratitude for the dogs I'd run through the snowy trails of the Chandalar River valley. And most of all, gratitude for the sheer miracle of having lived for so long in a place that reinvented my dreams. In the end, I would die, not separate from that place but a part of its endless cycle of life and death. Like the bear, the snow, and the wind itself, I was *part* of a greater thing. Whatever came next, that knowledge filled me with a quiet, unyielding peace.

By day 10, I was closer to death than I'd like to admit. My broken bones had begun to set in the most unnatural directions, more than a few of my wounds were raging with infection, and sores were forming on my filthy skin where I lay. Then, for the third time since the attack, a bush plane passed low overhead.

The pilot was Ben, the same guy who had flown over on day 7. Ben would later tell me that he could see camp clearly from the cockpit and that something seemed off: The runway had not been looked after, the doors of the fuel house were flapping wildly in the wind, the water pump I had initially brought down to the Kavik had been pulled downriver.

"*Kavik, you got your ears on? Sue, you there? Something's not right,*" he said. And then, by the grace of a higher power to which I will be forever grateful, Ben said, "*I'm coming in.*"

For a moment, I sat in stark disbelief and questioned whether the voice was real or if my mind was playing tricks on me after a week and a half or starvation, dehydration, and injury. For self-preservation, I refused to let myself open up to the possibility that I might be saved. Because if Ben didn't actually land on that runway, it certainly would have killed me. But when I heard the plane touch down, the door of the Cessna open, and Ben's footsteps run across the gravel runway, I knew I was saved.

Instantly, the oppressive mantle of fear and uncertainty that had defined my existence over the past ten days melted away. Tears welled up in my eyes as the door of the dining hall swung open and Ben gazed down upon me on the floor.

"Holy shit, Sue," he said. "What happened? Are…are you OK?"

In an act of grace and humanity I will never forget, Ben proceeded to clean me up. Then he found me some clean clothes to change into, and—now that daylight had faded and flying was no longer an option—fed me, watered me, and lifted me into my bed where I spent a fitful night. I was saved, but for perhaps the first time, the extent of my injuries was beginning to become clear. I was broken. I'd been saved, but I was broken.

At the crack of dawn the next morning, Ben carried me to the Cessna 206, gently placed me in the jump seat beside his, and took off. Although I'd become accustomed to its constant gnaw, the pain had grown more intense with each passing day. I could feel that things were horribly wrong with my body, and I doubted whether I would ever be the same. But as we sped down the runway and lifted off, I allowed myself the luxury of thinking I was actually going to live. We circled to the west to turn around and head south toward Fairbanks, and I looked down onto the tundra, where I spotted the remains of the beta lying in the snow, now picked apart by the elements and the relentless cycle of life that defined the Arctic.

Ben flew me the three hours south to Fairbanks, where a ride was waiting when we landed. A few minutes later I was in the Fairbanks Hospital, where, after a very quick assessment by the team of doctors and nurses waiting there, I was told I required medical attention they could not provide. In addition to the several badly infected punctures and lacerations, I also needed work on my legs, my arms, my hips, my spine, my face, and my shoulders. The two closest hospitals that could take me were in Seattle and Portland, so after calling Eddie and explaining what happened, we took off for Portland.

I ended up staying in the hospital in Portland for several months, where the physicians, nurses, and physical therapists did an admirable job of putting my broken body back together and getting me up on my feet again. Over that time, the extent of my injuries was quantified: spinal disk protrusion at multiple vertebrae; multiple fractures to my arms, legs, shoulders, and various bones in my face; two severely dislocated hips that required a surgical intervention known as an open reduction internal fixation; reconstruction of the soft tissues around my hips, including ligaments, tendons, and muscles; a severely dislocated shoulder that needed a shoulder reduction and subsequent traction to realign the joint; debridement and re-stitching of the significant lacerations to my head; and weeks of extensive antibiotic treatments to stave off the infection that had raged through my body like an invading army. On more than one occasion, the doctors looking after me told me I was lucky to be alive.

Of course, I knew they were right. Had it not been for Ben's intuition, I likely would have died on the dining hall floor. But in the months to come, I had an awful lot of time to reflect on what had happened to me. And the truth is, as fortunate as I was, luck had very little to do with the outcome of my showdown with the bear. Like much of life in the Arctic, reality was a brutal bedfellow: One lived and one died.

CHAPTER 9

UNBROKEN

When I first got to the hospital, I only felt relief, the kind that washes over you when you wake up somewhere clean and warm after staring death in the face…and Portland was a world away from the occasional brutality of life on the North Slope. The white hospital sheets, the steady beep of the monitors, the murmur of the medical staff who paraded in and out of my room, hell, even the food… It was all so soft and safe that I let myself sink into it. For the first time in what seemed like months, I wasn't scanning the horizon for predators or listening for the howl of the wind to gauge the coming weather. But as the novelty of those first few days wore off, relief began to give way to unease. I was trapped in that sanitary environment; the walls of my room began to close in on me. I felt like an animal in a cage. I was fed and cared for but restless.

Eventually I was released, but my road to recovery was nowhere near complete, and the medical team in Portland wanted to keep me close, so I went to the only place I felt at home outside Alaska: Loretta's house, where Eddie and Jesse were both still living. The three of them had been near-constant visitors to the hospital during my stay (Jennie was living in North Dakota with her partner and two young children), but my return to Loretta's struck a melancholic chord that took me by surprise.

I stood in the front entryway, my crutches pressing into the old oak floorboards of the house that once felt like my second home. The subtle scent of pine cleaner and something faintly earthy wafted toward me as my fingers tightened around the crutches, the weight of my former life pressing against my chest. I'd never lived here with Ed and the kids, but we'd spent enough time at Loretta and Jim's that I knew every inch of the place as if it were my own.

The living room looked almost the same as it had when I left, as if no time had passed whatsoever. The overstuffed couch still sagged slightly on one side, a cup of tea perched on a coaster atop the oak end table an indication that Loretta still spent much of her time sitting there. The fireplace mantle, slightly dustier than it once was, held the same family pictures that had been there for as long as I could remember. Suddenly, the memories began to rush through my head like a movie trailer, a flashing highlight reel of the places and moments that had made up our life together: Eddie pushing toy cars around on the floor of our first house as the kids climbed all over him. That rainy Saturday we stayed in and danced to old records, the room spinning around us. The countless nights when the world outside seemed so far away and his arms felt like the only safe place I'd ever known. Jennie's first date. Jesse's first baseball game. School assignments and movie rentals and dinners and hugs and tears and cuddles on the couch.

But as I stood there in the front entryway looking around the house of the only woman who'd ever mothered me with a sense of kindness and respect befitting that title, the tide of my heart began to turn and those golden memories were slowly replaced by darker ones, like a shadow creeping along a deserted street. Fights over things I couldn't remember. The endless nights I trudged off to work while Ed and the kids stayed home. That insidious loneliness and dissatisfaction, like ivy slowly strangling the edges of my heart. The claustrophobia that came with living in a world structured by time frames and expectations and to-do lists and extended family. The seizures. And ultimately, the realization that life held more for me than what we had together.

I swallowed hard and shifted uncomfortably, the aches in my broken body mirroring the ache in my chest. For a brief moment, I was reminded of the love we had…a moment later of what we had lost. If anyone knew that love wasn't always enough, it was me. *Love isn't always enough*, I mumbled to myself.

"What's that?" Ed said as he carried my bag inside to the guest room.

Taking a shaky breath, I let the memories settle, bittersweet and raw, and hobbled inside. "Nothing," I replied.

As mixed as my emotions may have been, there was something infinitely comforting about being with family while I recovered. Ed made dinner when I was in too much pain to take care of myself; Jesse and I went on long (slow) walks around the neighborhood, catching up on the thousand little things that had somehow become lost in the distance between our lives. Strangely enough, despite everything that had happened (like us getting divorced and me marrying another man), Ed and I still considered each other family. *It only has to make sense to us*, we used to say to one another. And somehow, it did.

That said, we never spoke about the possibility of me staying or of us getting back together. We all knew my place was in Alaska and Ed's was in Portland, and there were too many miles between the two to make a long-distance relationship viable. That doesn't mean we didn't have conversations about the future, because we did. Ed and Jesse were both very concerned about my safety and expressed their feelings about it every chance they got.

"I know you need to live in Alaska, but isn't there somewhere *closer* or *safer*?" Jesse asked one night over dinner.

"What if you hire a few people to live and work up there with you?" Ed asked one night as we shared a glass of whiskey. "That way if something happens you've got someone there to get help."

I understood where they were coming from. From what they told me, I looked more dead than alive when I first arrived at the hospital despite Ben the pilot's efforts to clean me up. It would have been a troubling sight for even the most hardened Northerner, but for a son and ex-husband to see their mother and former wife that way would have been almost too much to handle. And yet the more they asked, the more I felt a flicker of resistance deep inside me. I knew where my place was, and it certainly wasn't in Portland. Kavik wasn't just where I lived; it was where I existed, raw and unfiltered, in a way I never could anywhere else.

I couldn't explain to them the pull of the North, the way it had claimed my soul. Jesse had seen it; he knew as much as anyone that Alaska wasn't just a place, it was a part of me. So I listened to their questions, reassured them as best I could, and then told them in no uncertain terms that as soon as my broken body had sufficiently healed, I was headed back.

At the same time, it wasn't a decision I came to lightly. You don't live through a bear mauling without ruminating on your own place on the food chain, and every time I moved I was reminded of the lingering physical effects of the attack. My dislocated hips made it difficult to walk, my shoulders ached every time I tried to lift my arms over my head, my back was in near-constant pain, and the wounds on my head stubbornly refused to heal. Then, in the weeks that followed, I grappled with an untold host of psychological demons that visited my dreams with frightening regularity, not the least of which was the beta. One time I jolted out of bed in the middle of the night to find the bear perched over me, about to grab my head in its jaws once again. I screamed and reached for a gun that wasn't there and then thrashed around long and loud enough that Eddie came running into the room.

"Sue! *Sue!*" he called.

"The bear! The fucking bear!" I screamed back, my eyes wide and wild as I fought him, pounding my fists into his chest and face.

"Sue," he said more gently as he took me by the shoulders and brought me back to the present. "It's OK; I'm here." Ed wrapped his arms around me, spoke softly to me, and sat me back down on the bed as I woke up and realized where I was. Hyperventilating and sweating, I threw my arms around him and cried myself back to sleep.

Yet as my body healed, my resolve hardened. Every time I looked out the front window at the gray, rainy city, I felt a pang of longing for the wild expanse of the Arctic, for the sound of snow crunching under my boots, for the northern lights casting green shadows on the snowy ground. I thought of the bears and the wolves, the frost and the endless skies that stretched toward infinity all around me, and realized that I hadn't chosen Alaska because it was easy. I'd chosen it because it was where I felt most alive, even in the face of death.

Three months to the day after I arrived in Portland, I was given the green light by the doctors and physical therapists to resume "normal activities." The writing had been on the wall for quite a while, but now that I was officially cleared for duty, my future opened up before me like an open road. So the first thing I did was call Mike Tolbert. We'd been in touch off and on since the attack—he even came down to Portland to visit me—but I had never made my intentions clear to him until I got the thumbs-up from the medical team that had put me back together like Humpty Dumpty.

"Hey," he said. "How are you holding up?" There was a trepidation in his voice, perhaps a worry that he was going to have to start all over again with Kavik after I'd gotten *this close* to buying it.

"Better," I replied. "Listen, the doctors just cleared me for duty again. So I wanted to see what you think about me coming back."

He paused. "Well, Sue, we've done this dance before, and I know that once you set your mind to something, there's no turning you around. So if you think you can do it, you know I'll back you up."

He paused again, choosing his words carefully. "But if you can't, Sue, you gotta be honest with me…and with yourself. You've got nothing to prove. After what you've been through, no one would blame you for moving on. But if you're asking me whether I think you can handle it, you already know the answer."

This was it. The bear attack had been my crucible, the acid test to see if I was as tough, as resilient, and as independent as I'd always thought I was. Portland was *right there*; Eddie was *right there*; a life of stability and predictability and safety *right there* for me to claim once again as my own. In the Pacific Northwest, there'd be no more life-threatening cold and blizzards, no more months of darkness and solitude, no more bears waiting to use me as their launchpad for a higher spot in the merciless hierarchy that defined the animal kingdom.

The attack had taken so much from me, but the one thing that remained, as steadfast and as powerful as ever, was my connection to that land. Even then, I could feel its pull. I swallowed hard, the weight of the decision pressing on me. For months, I'd been trying to outrun what had happened and make peace with the fear. But I knew running wasn't the answer. If I didn't go back, I'd never know if I still had it in me.

"Mike," I said, "I'm ready."

Another pause followed, and I could almost hear his grin on the other end. "I'll book your flight." As I hung up, my heart pounded, but the thing rattling in my chest wasn't fear; it was determination. Kavik was waiting. And so was I.

Six days later, I was on a flight from Portland to Fairbanks, the next day on a bush plane north. As we crested the Brooks Range and the North Slope opened before us like an infinite canvas waiting for me to write my story, I felt a sense of peace and belonging as profound as anything I'd ever known. Before long, the tires rumbled to a stop on the airstrip.

I was home.

As determined as I was to make things feel normal, the first few days back at Kavik were surreal. More times than not I felt as though I was living in the third person, a casual observer of the *Story of Sue*. I was me and this was my life, only sometimes it wasn't.

Slowly I settled back into my routine. The camp had fallen into disrepair during my absence, and I threw myself into my work with vigor, if only because the hours kept the fear at bay. But as life took on a more predictable rhythm and I felt the blood of Alaska once again pump through my veins, I knew I had made the right decision in returning. I had long ago accepted the eventuality of my own death because it came with the territory—literally and figuratively. To live the lifestyle that I'd chosen, to live in the most remote corner of the world with only animals as your closest neighbors—to choose to be more animal than human, maybe—you have to be comfortable with your own death. I had no intention of going out and seeking my own demise, but I accepted that at some point it was coming.

When I was a little girl in Chicago, I spent a fair bit of time with my grandfather, a man we kids knew simply as "Bing." He wasn't particularly kind and always treated me as a much-older version of myself than I really was, but somehow I was regularly foisted off on him as he made his rounds around Chicago as a lumber salesman. During one of those trips, he said to me, for no reason in particular, "Don't stand on the railroad tracks if you don't want to get hit by a fucking train." Forty years later, there I was standing on the railroad tracks. I just hoped I'd hear the engine in time to jump off.

As part of that process, the first thing I had to do was make peace with the beta. I knew his body had long since been taken away by the wildlife officers, but the spot where he'd died was etched into my cranium like a childhood memory. So I shouldered my rifle, strapped a handgun to my waist, and walked out across the tundra to where our showdown ended, with only the full moon above and a headlamp on my head to show me the way.

When I got to the spot, I knelt down in the snow and whispered a prayer for the two creatures whose lives were forever changed by their fateful meeting that day. A part of me wanted to be infuriated, to rage and scream and wail for all that the beta had taken away from me. But I couldn't find those feelings. Instead, all I could do was give thanks for the life I'd been given and the opportunity to live it on my own terms once again. As for the bear, well, he was only doing what he was programmed to do, and I felt deep sorrow for having killed him.

After a few minutes, I stood up, brushed the snow off my knees, and reached into my pocket, where I found another heart rock, which I placed gently on top of the snow; somewhere below was the one I'd left on the bear's body a few months before. (I'd find them both there the following summer.) Then I turned around and walked back toward camp, leaving more and more of the attack behind with each step I took. The way I saw it, either I could let the attack define me or I could take control of my life once more and create my own reality. In the end, the choice was all too easy: My life was mine alone to define, and I'd never grant another living thing that power over me.

At the same time, I knew that if I let myself think about things too much—the second I hesitated when a bear or a wolf or any other predator set its sights on me—I was as good as dead. If I let the bear attack turn me into a second-guessing version of myself, I had no business being out there anymore. I may as well have let the beta finish the job because the outcome would eventually be the same. The wild north of Alaska is no place to doubt yourself… especially if you plan on surviving for any length of time. I walked back across the tundra, eventually crossing the river and into the front door of the dining hall.

"I'm back," I said to myself. Kavik might kill me one day, but it's where I belonged.

I'd only been back at camp for a few weeks, and the deep dark of winter held the land in an icy grip that refused to yield. I spent long hours sleeping and recovering my still-mending body, followed by stints of frenzied activity that saw me tend to the many things that needed to get done to keep the camp running smoothly. I still was far from a diesel mechanic, but years at Kavik had taught me more about small engine repair and equipment maintenance than I ever thought I'd need to know. Every day was an adventure and I made far more mistakes than I care to admit, but somehow I managed.

At the same time, I could feel the effects of the attack on my body. Parts of me that I'd never felt before hurt like hell, and I became exhausted by doing simple tasks that I once ripped through before lunchtime. Still, the fuel tanks needed to be monitored, the generators maintained, and the heaters cleaned. The snow needed to be cleared, the runway required constant upkeep, and the snow machines needed to be fueled and oiled and kept in working order. Supplies needed to be ordered, reservations needed to be taken, and every building needed to be checked on a regular basis for signs of damage or animal infiltration or burst water pipes or any of the hundred other things that could go wrong when temperatures dropped to minus forty degrees and lower. And nobody else was coming to do it.

I had embraced that reality years before, but no matter how long I'd lived at Kavik, it still gnawed at my psyche like a persistent termite: Even the simplest slip-up could have severe consequences. If I underestimated my fuel consumption or perhaps missed a leak in a fuel tank or line and found myself without heat in midwinter temperatures, there would be no Sue left once spring came around.

But as daunting as that kind of responsibility may have been, I never let it weigh me down. For at the end of every day, I stood out on the frozen land I'd made into my home; threw my arms out wide; gazed up at the aurora borealis painting the night sky a million shades of pink, purple, red, and green; and thanked my lucky stars for my life.

Sometimes that life threw curveballs I didn't see coming, though, like the afternoon I was gloriously lounging in bed in my jammies with a good book when an ungodly scream ripped through the camp. For a moment I thought it was a woman, but once I came back to Earth and realized there wasn't another human for several hundred miles, I recognized what it really was. Around Kavik, the only animal that could make that sound is a wolverine. And those were not screams of joy but the holy hell of pain and anger.

Solitary, powerful, and ornery as any animal I've ever encountered, wolverines are some of Alaska's most resilient and ferocious creatures. Compact and powerful, a wolverine resembles a bear, though quite a bit smaller at only around fifty pounds and approximately four feet in length from nose to tail. For a person living on her own in Alaska, though, by far the most critical characteristic of the wolverine is that given the right motivation, it will attack anything that pisses it off, no matter how big the opponent. So when the screams ripping through camp pushed me out the door to investigate, I did so as quietly as possible…and with a rifle in my hands.

I walked toward the back of camp to investigate, making sure to stay away from the screams as best I could, and soon figured out what had set the wolverine off: a massive snow drift beside the gen shed had allowed it to wander too close to a generator's exhaust pipe, which was usually several safe feet off the ground. As the wolverine walked by, it must have gotten a faceful of searing heat from the pipe, prompting it to instinctively clamp its formidable jaws on what it perceived to be an attacker and causing a kind of pain it had surely never experienced…hence its rage.

Lost in thought as I pieced together the mystery, I walked out from behind the shed and there, not more than fifty yards away and staring directly at me, was the wolverine. As soon as it caught me in its sight, it charged. Under different circumstances, I may have marveled at the animal's form as it approached with break-neck speed. With short legs and massive paws, wolverines have an unmistakable way of running, with a bounding, galloping rhythm that sees their backs hump up and down in an undulating pattern as their dark-brown fur ripples slightly, bushy tail streaming behind. But there was no time for such luxuries. There was nowhere to hide. I lifted the rifle to my shoulder.

"You son of a bitch," I said under my breath. "Don't you fucking dare."

I cracked a few shots in the charging animal's direction, hoping I wouldn't piss it off even more. Luckily, the sound of the gun and the wall of snow kicked up by the bullets were enough to convince the wolverine I wasn't worth the effort, and it quickly turned around and headed away toward the northeastern edge of camp, where copses of low willows eventually disappeared into the hills a few miles beyond. Given that small window of opportunity, I followed the wolverine toward the safety of the dining hall, where I quickly retreated.

I didn't sleep much the rest of that night but instead kept a wary ear attuned to every sound in camp. Wolverines have a vengeful streak that makes them formidable adversaries, and I didn't want to underestimate it. Mardy had taught me that as homey and comfortable as the dining hall may have felt, it offered virtually no protection against the claws of a determined animal.

The next morning there was no further sign of the wolverine in camp, so I cautiously returned to my daily routine, though always with a gun in tow and always on the lookout for a flash of brown fury headed my way. I slept better as the days went by, though I was still restless. Every crunch of snow was either an angry wolverine or a bear with an agenda, and I was bowed under a lingering sense of vulnerability I'd rarely felt before.

But time heals all wounds, and as the days following the encounter turned into weeks and then months, I began to take a more practical view of the situation. Though fierce at times, wolverines are largely solitary and tend to avoid humans unless provoked... even by a marauding exhaust pipe. Still, I began each trip outside my front door in much the same way, by first examining camp for tracks or other signs of the wolverine. I never went outside without a weapon; even my forays to the outhouses back by The Boneyard were accompanied by a handgun in a holster, which I held dutifully in my hands as I did my business.

Eventually the fear I'd been holding on to subsided into a wary respect. Under normal circumstances, I likely wouldn't have given the wolverine much thought after it ran off across the tundra that afternoon. But as much as I hated to admit it, the bear attack had changed me. I still had confidence that I could handle myself in an encounter, and the fact that I was able to lift the rifle to my shoulder as the wolverine charged and shoot at it without injuring it or killing it was a testament to that fact. But at the same time, it was a reminder to me that my life at Kavik often balanced precariously on the edge of existence.

At the end of the day, I was reminded how small and fragile humans are in such a massive, raw, and untamed place. My solitude came with myriad rewards named and unnamed, but at the price of certain risks. At the same time, that sense of vulnerability only served to increase the kinship I felt with the land and its creatures. Each sunrise and moonlit night, each bay of a lone wolf, each time the ground thundered under the hooves of a thousand caribou felt a little more precious, if only because it was marked by the recognition that life on the tundra is never guaranteed, only borrowed.

As 2009 wound on and spring turned to summer and fall once again, I was reminded that the uncomfortable balance between life and death doesn't only happen in the world's far-flung places. It had been more than a year since the bear attack and my subsequent rehabilitation in Portland, but I was missing my family and made plans to head back down to spend Thanksgiving with Eddie, Jesse, and Loretta for a couple of weeks before winter settled over Kavik in earnest and I would be on my own for the next few months. With a clear forecast for the foreseeable future, I battened everything down and kept my fingers crossed. But the storm that awaited me outside was far worse than any one hundred-miles-per-hour wind.

I called Eddie from the Anchorage airport, if only to update him on my progress. We'd been through enough north–south rodeos together to know that King Weather could scuttle the best-laid plans on a moment's notice, but the skies were clear and my flight on time.

"See you in a few hours," I said.

"Can't wait."

Once I arrived, I made my way outside to the passenger pickup lanes, where Eddie and I had agreed to meet, but there was no sign of him. I called, but there was no answer. Frustrated, I called Jesse.

"Mom," he said. "Dad's gone."

Perhaps it didn't register with me that Jesse's voice sounded further away than I'd ever heard before, so I stupidly replied, "OK, I'll go back outside and wait for him."

"No, Mom," he said, his voice breaking. "Dad's *gone*. After you two hung up the phone this morning, he had a heart attack. He's gone."

The air was sucked from my lungs, and the world began to swim. I'd lived through more births and deaths than I could remember, but this was an eventuality I'd never considered. It couldn't be true; there must have been some kind of mistake. Some macabre and eternally fucked-up part of me waited for Jesse to start laughing and say, "Kidding! He's running a bit late, that's all."

But nothing came. Jesse's word hung in the air between us, and all I could do was mumble "OK" as the tears began to stream down my face. "I'll…I'll get a cab."

The rest was a blur. Somehow I made it to Loretta's, where I was almost immediately sucked into the vortex that surrounds the business of dying. Beyond the near-constant phone calls and the meetings and the insurance and the arrangements and the making sure that everyone else was taken care of, there was little room left to simply collapse into myself and mourn. On those rare occasions where I found time to be alone with my thoughts, though, I had a few realizations.

Most importantly, you have to let people know how you feel about them while they're still here. Don't ever be scared to tell someone you love them because they may be gone before you know it and you'll wake up and realize you blew your chance. Also, don't fool yourself into thinking there's going to be time at the end to mend the wobbly fences between you and the people you care about. Time can be a fickle bitch. And when it runs out, the painful lessons you learn in those moments will tear a hole in your universe.

I wasn't always the best wife to Eddie. I am an unmitigatedly logical and analytical creature; expressing my emotions is not my forte. I didn't always appreciate him as much as I could have. I worked too much when we were together, stayed away too long when we weren't. Eddie wasn't perfect, either, but I loved him for his faults, as he did me for mine. And aren't we all in a position to be better to others, especially the ones we love? Tone it down a little here and there? But the irony of death is that I didn't realize any of that until it was too late.

Eddie and I always thought it would be me who went first. The lighthouse keeper, the hunter, the bear beater, the traveler, the ice walker, the lonely fairy child of the Alaskan wilderness. *She* was the one who was gonna go first. Not Eddie. Not Solid Ed, my nice guy, my family man, my love. But life had other plans. In the end, the painful universal truth is that life turns out exactly the way it's supposed to but seldom how you think it will. Go ahead and make your plans and dream the dream of lovers. But life will have its way. It isn't personal, though sometimes it sure fucking feels that way.

In the end, we all knew that even after Eddie's death, my time in Portland would come to an end sooner than later. Yes, a part of me was torn between grief and the need to be strong for Loretta,

Jesse, and Jennie, but I soon realized there was little need. As much as I hated to admit it, Loretta's fate was in the hands of her other children. Jesse (who had decided to move in with Megan) was strong, confident, and capable, and I had no doubt that he'd be able to forge his place in the world despite the loss of his dad. Jennie was a wife and mother, and with two young children to care for and a house in another state, her life was elsewhere.

Two weeks after Eddie passed, I was on a plane back to Kavik, where I would try to mend my broken heart. I was bent with sorrow. Ed had been an anchor in my life, a solid and steadying force that I could always count on to be *there*, no matter how far away I was or how outlandish my plans. *Want to move away and run dogs? Sure thing! Need to marry another guy? I understand.* Only now he was gone.

After a brief stop in Fairbanks, I hopped on a bush plane headed to Kavik. As I'd done so many time before, I watched the city I'd come to know so well disappear beneath me as we struck a course due north over the broad, white landscape that had forever staked a claim in my heart. But as we flew, another feeling began to rise in my gut, slowly edging its way like snaky tendrils into the sorrow that had infiltrated my soul the previous two weeks: gratitude. Ed's death had been the worst thing that had ever happened to me, but I was so goddamn thankful for the time we got to share together. I'd never have him to tether my existence to reality, but I would hold on to those memories like a lifeline.

Over the course of the next winter, I found solace in the vastness and peace of my Arctic playground. The crack of the river as it heaved and groaned with changes in the weather, the flutter of ptarmigan wings as they carved a low arc in the sky when disturbed, the whisper of a wind that started a thousand miles away and blew across the hills to their indefinite end were my constant companions during that difficult time, and I threw myself headfirst into my Kavik life to dull the pain. Nature, like always, was my respite from a world of people and institutions I had a hard time navigating.

And while my heart certainly wanted the world to pause and mourn with me, life continued its endless ebb and flow unabated. Most times those patterns were beautiful, but often they showed me the realties and difficulties of the life I had chosen: shortages of food, fuel, and water that left me wondering if I would survive until the next bush plane graced my runway; equipment breakdowns that threatened to turn the camp cold and dark in a time when temperatures bottomed out at minus one hundred degrees… and of course that old son of a bitch Mardy, who seemed as determined as ever to bring me down.

Yet through it all, I never lost sight of what it was that brought me to Kavik in the first place. I loved life there because I was an active participant in my own existence, my success or failure in my own hands. Was it scary? Sometimes. Was it difficult? Absolutely. But in the end, it was all mine. Then, as always, I did what I wanted, when I wanted, where I wanted, and how I wanted. And that's *just* how I wanted it. And with that reality etched firmly into my cranium, I continued to forge through the rigors of my daily life with a shit-eating grin on my face.

CHAPTER 10

LIFE BELOW ZERO

The first winter after Eddie's death slowly turned to spring, and like most winters before, I had seen very few souls except for the bush pilots—including my savior, Ben—who made occasional pit stops at Kavik for fuel. Reveling in that solitude, I took the opportunity to make long snowmobile trips across the tundra, the machine's rubber track churning the snow underneath into a predictable pattern as I sped away from camp and away from the pain, toward an open horizon of hope and possibility ahead.

Those days were my respite and my salvation because even as the cold spring air bit against my face, there was a subtle softness to the breeze, a hint of earth and thaw and life to come as the sun cast a golden shadow over the ridges and hummocks that stretched endlessly before me. To the untrained eye, the land would have seemed desolate and lifeless, but to me the subtle changes of rebirth were everywhere: small buds beginning to appear on the willows, a trickle of water in an anonymous stream, the occasional patch of exposed tundra peeking through the snowy mantle that had covered it since October.

My destination of choice that spring was the Canning River, which was set inside a long, wide, and fertile valley that sprang from the heart of the Brooks Range and continued its journey before terminating at the Arctic Ocean some forty miles to the north of Kavik. As I made my way east, crossing the innumerable streams and tundra ponds that separated Kavik and the Canning, I felt my heart loosen and my spirit soar as the machine bounced beneath me. I had come to the Arctic for solitude and grace, and those springtime adventures offered every bit of that. At the same time, though, the roar and power of the snowmobile were thrilling, and I basked in its ability to take me longer and farther than my feet ever could.

No matter how often I made the trip, when I crested the final hill and gazed down into that magical valley, it took my breath away. To my right, the peaks of the Brooks Range rose dramatically in the distance, jagged spears punctuating the spring sky like a legion of Roman soldiers. Directly ahead, the valley stretched for miles across the broad expanse of the riverbed, much wider than my neighbor, the Kavik. The river was still locked in ice, but the open water glistening on its edges told me that breakup would not be far off.

When that happened, the landscape around the river would be transformed from one of frozen slumber to utter chaos, as feet-thick floes of ice, broken loose by warmer days and the movement of water underneath, collided in a symphony of sight and sound as they were carried downstream. It was at once thunderous and beautiful, a never-ending barrage of cracking, rumbling, and hissing as massive pieces slammed into one another, rose up like angry muskoxen on a mountain pass, and then settled back down again into the churning water underneath, now painted a turgid brown with the silt and debris carried downriver from the mountains beyond.

Along the bank, a twisted array of ice lay in a jumbled mess, some pieces no bigger than my hand, others larger than a car. The ones not dredged in river mud shone with a deep, iridescent blue that spoke of the months of cold that had created them, one tiny layer at a time, each one telling its own story of life in the Arctic. Overhead, ducks and geese—just returning after many months away—circled against a brilliant blue backdrop as a distant herd of caribou, their coats now shaggy with tufts of shedding fur as they prepared for the warmth to come, moved slowly across the valley floor as they foraged for food among the widening patches of vegetation.

Sitting there astride my snowmobile, I couldn't help but marvel at the undeniable force of nature. It was thrilling and humbling, and while it made me feel immeasurably small and insignificant, at the same time I felt more alive than I'd ever been. Eddie was gone and my body would bear the scars of the bear attack for the rest of my days, but I was alive and in the only place I wanted to be at that moment. I opened my thermos, poured myself a steaming cup of coffee, and soaked in every sound, every sight, every smell. It hadn't been easy to say goodbye to Jesse and Jennie and return to the North, but I knew in that moment that I'd made the right decision.

After lingering there, alone but not alone, on that high bank for what seemed like a minute but was more like several hours, I fired up the snowmobile again and turned back toward Kavik, a ride that would take two and a half hours. As the machine rumbled over the snow, the setting sun to the northwest bathed me and the land around me in ever-deepening shades of pink and blue. Later I pulled into Kavik, greeted the foxes that regularly skirted the edges of camp, and walked toward the dining hall. I was tired, windburned, and sore, but my mind was quiet, my soul at ease. Little did I know that in two weeks' time something would happen that would flip my world upside down once again.

Later that summer, I opened my email (yes, I had internet, thanks to a satellite system I'd installed several years before) and was surprised to find a message from a Fox News reporter named

Greta Van Susteren. Through some bizarre twist of fate I still don't understand, she had heard about my life at Kavik and wanted to come interview me in my native habitat alongside former Alaska governor Sarah Palin. Something about *strong Alaskan women*, she said. The interview aired without incident (I actually didn't see it at the time), but Sarah and I hit it off from the start. She shared my unorthodox sense of humor, and we had both been captivated by Alaska's untamed beauty for decades, finding a reflection of our own adventurous spirits in its vast wilderness.

During that meeting, Sarah informed me that she was in the process of shooting her own reality TV show—*Sarah Palin's Alaska*—and wanted to include Kavik (and me) in one of the episodes. It was as odd a request as any I'd ever had, but I liked Sarah and I didn't see much harm in participating in the show. So on a breezy late-summer day in 2010, Sarah, her father Chuck, and his good friend Steve flew into Kavik, which they would use as their home base for the next several days as they ventured into the nearby hills to hunt caribou.

My role in the entire operation was minimal, and (like with so many of my guests) I primarily provided logistical support in the form of food, shelter, warmth, and water. I was only on camera for a minute or two and mostly talked about the bear attack, but something about my personality, lifestyle, and worldview resonated with a wider audience than anyone anticipated. (I'd later learn that my statement *Some girls want perfume and diamonds. Blood, guts, and bullets…that's me* was what really made people notice.) Either way, it wasn't long after that episode aired that I received another email from a different producer, this one at the helm of a program called *Flying Wild Alaska*, a reality program that chronicled the life and times of the Tweto family and their small family-run airline, Era Alaska.

My involvement in *Flying Wild Alaska* was still nominal, but I appeared on several episodes. Once again, though, the world proved to be a much smaller and much stranger place than I thought because as *Flying Wild Alaska* was still in production, the executive producer of the show, a gentleman named Tommy Baynard, sat me down at Kavik one night and blew me away.

"What do you think about a show where your life is the principal story?" he asked as we sat around the dining hall drinking whiskey.

I choked on my drink, if only because the idea was probably the most outlandish thing I'd ever heard. I mean, I've never been Shirley Temple material (the bleep button was probably invented with me in mind), but there was an earnestness in Tommy's voice that made me realize he wasn't joking.

"C'mon, Tommy, get a grip. Reality TV isn't made for women like me."

He laughed. "I've never been more serious," he said, looking into his glass and swishing the ice around. "Listen, you're not like anyone I've ever met, and people *love* you. You're raw. You're untamed. You don't give a holy shit what people think about you, and you do what you want. You're an inspiration, Sue, and I believe people will eat that up." I scowled.

"But if it makes you feel any better," he continued, "the show wouldn't be only about you. I'd like to chronicle the lives of several people living on their own terms in Alaska. You'd be a big part of the show…just not the only part."

I was equal parts shocked and intrigued. Like all northern operations, Kavik was exceedingly expensive to run. The cost of fuel, food, and other goods was staggeringly higher than elsewhere because it *all* had to be flown in. Bottled water, canned tuna, toilet paper, flour—even the bullets I used for protection and hunting—every last thing arrived in Kavik via my airstrip, which meant it cost five to ten times more than it would anywhere else in the state. At the same time, my income stream was unpredictable, highly specialized, and dependent upon the whims of King Weather. If the scientists and exploration companies who came to Kavik decided to stay for an extended period, I could be flush with cash. If they looked elsewhere, on the other hand, my accounts could easily run into the red, which they often did. Because of that, the idea of securing another source of income was appealing.

"OK, well, you've got me interested," I said.

Tommy smiled and stood up; it was getting late. "Awesome. Let me take the idea to some people I know in LA. I'll let you know once I have a better idea of the appetite for such a thing, if any."

The next morning, Tommy was on a bush plane headed south. As always, I stood beside the runway and watched the plane disappear over the horizon, ultimately just a glint of sunlight against the infinite Alaskan sky. As much as I've always enjoyed being on my own, I usually felt a tinge of sadness when visitors left camp, and that day was no different. But there was something else stirring inside me that morning too, a nervousness that change was in the air.

Not long after he left, Tommy called. His idea about the show had been warmly received by his most trusted friends, enough so that he wanted to return to Kavik with a business associate in tow. Together they hoped to outline the show in greater detail, shoot some footage for prospective investors, and generally gauge my appetite for embarking on what might well amount to a life-changing commitment. I hadn't signed on any dotted lines and figured it was a long shot at best, but I've never been one to shy away from a challenge, so two weeks later I welcomed Tommy and his colleague Tim back to camp.

It was early fall, high season at Kavik, and I was buzzing with the myriad responsibilities that the season demanded. In between, Tommy, Tim, and I grabbed snippets of conversation, during which they asked me more questions about my life and my beliefs. Later one evening, when the hikers and paddlers and birdwatchers and naturalists had retired to their cabins for the night, we settled in for a few nips of fifteen-year-old Laphroaig, where—as my tongue loosened and the stories flowed—something magical happened. Before the evening was out, they had cobbled together the foundation of the show that would change my life, *Life Below Zero*.

Over the next couple of days, the producers hammered out a series of "sizzle reels," short proof-of-concept promotional video clips of me doing things around camp that were intended to grab the attention of producers, networks, and/or investors and convince them to green-light the project. Days later they returned to LA to fine-tune the idea and see if they could sell the show. It would be months before I heard from Tommy again, months where the short, glorious Alaskan autumn turned quickly to winter and I was once again on my own, with just the snow and the wind and the animals to keep me company. As excited as I was at the initial idea of the show, the months of solitude had turned my head to the daily tasks of my survival, and I'd given it little thought since. But when Tommy called again in late December, his voice reminded me that while I'd been going about the machinations of my daily existence, someone else was trying to sell the concept of my life (and others) as gripping TV.

After exchanging pleasantries, Tommy dropped a fifty-megaton bomb on my life. "Sue," he said, "we found someone to back our idea. So if you're still interested, we are all systems go." I was flabbergasted. The idea of the show had been a fun distraction, but I *never* thought it would actually happen. "I… Let me think on it for a while," I said. "I'll get back to you in a couple of weeks."

What followed was a soul-searching session of Shakespearean proportions. I had always considered the idea of the show nothing more than a pipe dream, but here it was, a reality. In the days to come, I batted around an almost infinite, ever-changing list of pros and cons in my head and my heart. First there were the practical concerns. A predictable income would be nice, but I knew *nothing* about reality TV or the effect it would have on my life. How much time would filming take? Would it interfere with my responsibilities? Were there any liability issues I needed to consider?

Much more significant than those, however, were the personal and ethical questions Tommy's proposal had sparked. I had lived much of my life on my own, and the thought of having my day-to-day activities on display was unsettling. Just how much of my life would be shown? And if I did agree, how would the show portray me? I'd heard horror stories of people who had been on reality TV and been made to look like buffoons. I trusted Tommy wholeheartedly but really had no idea how much creative control he'd have over the final product…and the last thing I wanted was to become a caricature.

After multiple conversations, Tommy allayed my fears, and I decided to give the show a try. He was earnest about maintaining authenticity and honestly seemed to believe that by putting my life on display I may just inspire others to live their lives on their own terms too. In turn, I would gain the financial stability that Kavik had never afforded me. During our last conversation, though, I made sure to lay out some very specific boundaries about what I needed from the relationship.

"Remember one thing," I told Tommy and Tim as we chatted over coffee in the dining hall the morning the plane was set to come take him out. "I live out here because I'm not all there. I like my life and don't want this to kill what I have.

"I don't need to be a billionaire, and I'm monumentally worried about the hassle that comes with doing a show," I continued. "I wear Levi's 501s, smoke like it's a dying art form"—I've since quit—"and wear white V-neck T-shirts. If you can handle all that, then let's do it. I don't mind if you film what I do, but I don't want it to be crazy. Don't make it something it's not, and I don't want somebody up in my grill all the time."

Tommy smiled and nodded the whole time and then, after studying me for a good long time, finally reached out and shook my hand. "Sue," he said, "you've got yourself a deal. Let's make this into something special."

And so *Life Below Zero* was born.

Months later, I stood in the terminal of the Fairbanks airport and waited to meet the film crew for the first time. I had wanted our initial encounter to be in camp, but life had other plans for me. So when my previously broken leg and foot (I had fallen off the roof of one of the trailers in camp) began to give me trouble and required surgery, I headed down to Fairbanks for the procedure and subsequent rehabilitation. A couple of months later, there I was, waiting for four complete strangers—two camera operators, a director, and a producer—to herald the beginning of the next chapter of my life.

I had been preparing myself emotionally for their arrival for several weeks, although I still had no idea what our moment-to-moment and day-to-day interactions would look like. But Tommy had told me, "Just be yourself; they'll do the rest," so that's what I intended to do.

Our first week together was as bizarre as any I've ever experienced. Although they didn't sleep in my hotel room, the crew arrived bright and early each morning to film *all* my daily activities, from brushing my teeth (thrilling!) to talking on the phone. And when I drove north along the entire five-hundred-mile length of the Haul Road from Fairbanks to Deadhorse on the Arctic Ocean, where I would hop on a bush plane for the short forty-five-mile flight in to Kavik, they were right there with me as well. Suddenly, my once-anonymous life had turned into lenses and microphones and small cameras mounted on bush-plane instrument panels. And when the aircraft circled low over Kavik to give me an idea of the camp's condition before we landed, the cameras were right there as well, documenting my every move.

To that point, the experience had been surreal, almost comical. But to have them in Kavik—my sanctuary against an outside world I was happy to visit and even more excited to leave—was a completely different animal. So as the skis of the plane skidded to a stop on the snow-covered runway, I immediately began to have second thoughts. We hadn't even stepped into the dining hall for the first time together, and I was already feeling intruded on. My autonomy—the thing I prized most in the world—had suddenly evaporated. With the crew there, I could no longer sleep for twenty-four or thirty-six consecutive hours (not exactly gripping television), and my otherwise peaceful surroundings would now be filled with the unfamiliar hum of technology and people. The rhythm of my life was set to change dramatically, and I was as protective as I was curious.

Luckily, the crew was professional and eager to learn. In the three weeks that followed, they walked me through every step of the sometimes-uncomfortable process that accompanied turning my life into cinematic entertainment. Lots of that edification had to do with the minutiae of filming in the harshest climate on Earth. Where we really got an education, though, was in learning how to deal with one another.

For one thing, Kavik was no *Survivor* tropical island, and two of the crew had never experienced Alaskan weather. Suddenly I had become responsible for not only my own well-being but that of complete strangers too. The cultural gaps between LA and Kavik were difficult to bridge too. You see, it's one thing to say you want to film some crazy lady living on her own in Alaska but quite another when you come face-to-face with what that life actually entails.

For example, since I had been away from Kavik for three months, it would take a few days for me to get camp running smoothly and the accommodation trailers ready to host guests, which meant the crew had to sleep on the dining hall floor in the interim. Meanwhile, a family of tundra voles—small, mouse-like rodents that inhabit the area and are active year-round—had taken advantage of my absence and decided that the warmth of the dining hall was much safer and more luxurious than the outside world of winter. I hadn't yet caught sight of the critters, but signs of their activity were everywhere, and I knew it was only a matter of time before what began as a small problem would turn into a significant infestation. As cute as they are, voles are vigorous chewers and would gnaw their way through everything in the dining hall, from food to wires to the tent itself, not to mention my precious food supplies. Something had to be done, and quickly. The longer I waited, the greater chance they'd have to establish themselves, wreaking a whole different kind of havoc on my life.

With no hardware store down the street selling vole traps, I had to lean on two of my closest friends—ingenuity and gunpowder—for help. I drilled a few two-inch holes in the bottom of a small trash can, set it on top of a small pile of lumber near the spot of the voles' greatest activity, and filled it with enough peanut butter to choke a small bear. I didn't just want the voles to run in and grab their food, I wanted them to remain there for as long as possible while they feasted. Then, after everyone else had gone to sleep, I lay down and waited.

When I had listened long enough to know that the trash can was now full of what I suspected was every vole that had invaded my space, I picked up the .410 shotgun I'd placed nearby, tiptoed over to the trash can, and unloaded a few rounds into their midst. The dining hall flashed orange with each shot, the sound echoed through the building like thunder, and the wood underneath what was once the bottom of the trash exploded into a shower of splinters. I'll admit it was a brutish way to deal with the problem, but a vole's reproductive proclivities are nothing to be trifled with.

Shocked, the crew flew out of their sleeping bags and into the now-smoky hallway where I'd set the trap. Their eyes were wide with shock and terror as they observed the scene, me standing there with a shotgun in my hands, a now-shredded trash can filled with the remains of the vole family.

"What the hell is going on?" one yelled.

"Just doing a little pest control," I answered, proud of my quick thinking and speedy resolution to what could have been a significant problem. But as I looked across their confused faces, now washed with disbelief, I realized they were anything but reassured. *What have we gotten ourselves into?* their expressions said.

"Welcome to Kavik," I said. "Guess you're not in Kansas anymore."

To their infinite credit, the crew took their abrupt introduction to my world in stride. At the same time, I knew as they wandered back to bed and muttered among themselves that the vole incident had been a grim reminder to them that things at Kavik did not operate the way they did in the rest of the world. Where we would go from there, though, was anybody's guess.

After the vole eradication, things between the crew and me slowly improved. We spent an awful lot of time together, and I eventually became accustomed to their near-constant presence in my life (though having my every action filmed never stopped being weird). With time we even grew friendly with one another, sitting together in the dining hall having late-night drinks and swapping stories of our lives. That said, the crew changed regularly, as different members of the group either left the company or were needed on other projects. That gave me a fairly steady stream of people I needed to introduce to the Kavik way of life, an introduction that occasionally saved them from harm. One of those times occurred a few years into filming (at which point *Life Below Zero* had somehow become a reality TV sensation), when an eager cameraman let his zeal cloud his judgment.

For as long as I could remember, almost every year I'd been at Kavik had seen one or two hibernating bears wake up in the middle of the winter, expel the fecal plug that otherwise blocked their gastrointestinal tract during months of dormancy, and emerge, ravenous, from their dens, only to find a world covered in snow. And for a grizzly bear on the North Slope, a world covered in snow is a world with very limited food sources.

In my experience, every time this happened, the bear went "rogue," a semi-crazed state where its behavior was erratic and dangerous and almost maniacally focused on the procurement of food. At the same time, the wolves around Kavik know a rogue bear without a consistent food source is a weak bear. Once the wolves spot the bear, all they have to do is keep it running for a few miles before the bear's limited energy stores give out and the pack can take it down.

As it happens, the crew was in camp at the same time a rogue bear was crashing its way through Kavik in search of food while simultaneously being stalked by a local wolf pack. Excited at the possibility of Emmy-worthy footage, the cameraman stood up, grabbed his gear, and headed toward the door.

"Where are you going?" I asked.

"I gotta get out there and film this," he replied excitedly.

"Hold on a second, bucko," I said as I strapped on a headlamp, holstered my Ruger, and walked to the door with him. "We really don't know what's going on out there, and you could be putting yourself in more danger than you know."

"But you just said the bear's on the other side of camp."

"Follow me," I said.

We walked outside into the dark of Arctic night, around the

corner of the dining hall, where I shone a flashlight on the bear, who was back in The Boneyard. As I did, my light also illuminated two sets of yellow eyes nearby. "You see those?" I said. "Those are the two lead wolves. Those are the ones that *want* to be seen."

Then I turned to the left and pointed the light toward the brush on the far side of camp, beyond the runway. "But what you don't see are the fourteen sets of eyes over there. Those are the ones that will take the bear out, the same ones that may have taken you out if you came out here in the dark on your own. So let's just go back inside and let the wolves do what they're meant to do."

And so my life became a Ping-Pong match of extremes. For weeks at a time, I'd have a camera documenting every breath I took, followed by the intense solitude that only life in the Arctic can bring. I was certainly at peace when on my own, but at the same time there was an undeniable thrill that accompanied the crew's visits.

Meanwhile, the show grew more popular with each passing season and was received with critical acclaim by the powers that be in Hollywood. In 2016, *Life Below Zero* won its first Emmy award for Outstanding Cinematography for a Reality Program, an award it would go on to win seven more times, making it the record holder for most Emmy wins for best cinematography in reality television history. For me, that meant regular trips to La-La Land for award shows, parties, and interviews on national television, where the enigma woman from the Far North would hoist her boobs skyward, slip into a designer dress and a pair of Jimmy Choos, and talk about a life nobody else could fathom.

The show's notoriety trickled down to its principal characters, and as one of them I became more well-known than I ever thought possible, a turn of events I found as thrilling as it was threatening. For one thing, there was a profound sense of gratitude and validation, as the audience seemed to find inspiration in my lifestyle, my struggles, and my no-nonsense approach to my own existence. And as affected as it may sound, I honestly believed the show afforded me the opportunity to bring Alaska—the most insanely beautiful place I'd ever lived—to a wider audience of people who might never have gotten the chance to visit.

At the same time, there was an underlying sense of unease and vulnerability that accompanied every visit by the crew to Kavik, no matter how long we'd known each other and how many episodes we'd shot. Would this be the time they made me look the fool? I also had to contend with the scrutiny and criticism that invariably accompany notoriety, and my once deeply private existence drew comments from people who knew nothing about me. Most were supportive, but haters *loved* to rain on my parade. I exaggerated the dangers of my lifestyle. I was a terrible hunter. I wasn't a *real* Alaskan. And on and on and on. But I'd learned many years before to let go of the things that hurt me, and the comments rolled away like water off a duck's back. In the end, I focused on the positives that the show brought to my life and the real connections it helped me make with people I'd never have otherwise met. Like Mikayla.

Eight-year-old Mikayla was a real fan of mine, and when that precious little angel was diagnosed with cancer and asked if there was any place on Earth she wanted to go, she immediately chose Kavik. So in conjunction with the Make-A-Wish Foundation, her parents and I arranged for her to visit. But when Mikayla's condition worsened and a trip to Kavik became too much for her little body to bear, we compromised and had her go to Fairbanks instead.

In the meantime, I worked with my connections there to make the trip everything Mikayla had dreamed it would be. We had reindeer, northern lights, dogsleds, airplane rides, and even a special visit from Santa Claus himself. In a life where her horizon had become filled with shades of darkness, little Mak enjoyed a few days of light and love…all because I was on TV. And when Mikayla eventually left the world and my heart was torn to shreds, I found a modicum of comfort in knowing that I'd helped make her last days special. Months afterward, her parents came to Kavik and we spread her ashes over the land she loved but never got to see. Now a part of her lives there forever.

The same can be said for the many viewers who realized the important place that heart-shaped rocks have played in my life. For as long as I can remember, I've placed them in memory of people and events worthy of commemoration. Fans caught on to it and somehow or another began to ask me to place them around Kavik in memory and support of their loved ones. *My dad just passed. My aunt is sick. My husband was wounded fighting overseas.*

Sometimes, the messages brought me to tears. *Hi Sue. My dad and I used to watch* Life Below Zero *together. And it meant so much to me because that was time that we had together. We knew we were never going to get to Alaska, but we watched the show religiously, and now that he's gone, I can't help but think of those precious moments we shared while watching you.*

In every case, I tried to honor the person by writing their name on a heart rock and setting it in a small, protected area in the braided bed of the Kavik River. It wasn't the Sistine Chapel, but if my small efforts could make a difference in someone's life, I was honored to do it.

Sometimes, though, the river flooded. When that happened, even my sanctuary wasn't safe from the forces of nature, and the heart rocks I'd placed got washed away. But rather than feel sadness when that happened—which it invariably did—the rising waters actually filled me with a sense of hope and of renewal.

Eventually, I thought, *nature will always take back what is hers.*

CHAPTER 11

THE HUNTER AND THE HUNTED

Since my earliest days as a girl trying to survive on her own in Alaska, hunting has been as important a part of my life as breathing itself. Whether you agree with the philosophy or not, the reality of living a remote life is that fresh fruit and vegetables are scarce and flying food in on airplanes cost-prohibitive. I'd say it's kill or be killed, but the truth is it's more like hunt or die...and I've never cottoned much to the idea of a premature death, no matter how often it's come for me. In the interim, I've eaten just about every creature that walks, swims, or flies. But it hasn't always been easy or predictable. And the first time I did it, just a twelve-year-old girl pointing a rifle at a deer for the first time, it was downright heart-wrenching.

I remember the day like it was yesterday. The late winter wind whispered through the trees, stinging my cheeks as I crouched low in the brush, gun in hand. I'd been outside for hours and the cold had settled deep in my bones, but I tried to ignore it and focus instead on the delicate, purposeful tracks in the snow before me. Meanwhile, my stomach clenched, a combination of persistent hunger and the gravity of what I'd set out to do. I'd learned a variety of ways to feed myself—not all of them dignified—but knew that if I could master the art of hunting, it would open a door to survival like nothing else could, likely for the rest of my life.

I moved slowly and intentionally, mindful of keeping my steps light and placing my feet where the snow was firmest to avoid crunching underfoot. "They'll hear you before they see you," Carl the bus driver had said. "And they'll smell you before they hear you." So I stayed downwind as I walked, my scent carried away behind me.

Through the trees, I finally spotted my prey: A young buck, not yet fully grown but certainly large enough to sustain me for weeks, grazed in a small clearing, its ears flicking instinctively with the slightest sound, its breath condensing to mist in the air. My heart was racing, pounding so hard in my chest I was sure the deer could sense it, if not hear it. I raised the rifle slowly, steadying it against my shoulder as I looked down the sight. My fingers felt clumsy, numb from the cold. I exhaled slowly, the way Carl had taught me, lining up the shot just behind the buck's shoulder where the heart sits, and squeezed the trigger.

The crack of the rifle shattered the silence. The deer jolted, stumbled a few awkward steps through the snow, and then crashed to the ground. Shaking, I lowered the gun. I'd killed it.

Pulling the trigger was just the beginning, though. Carl had taken the time to explain to me the steps involved in skinning and gutting the animal, and I knew what was to come would require as much effort as, if not more than, the hunt itself. My legs felt unsteady as I approached the buck, its body still, its dark eyes open and glassy as it stared into the great beyond. Guilt knotted in my stomach, at the same time twisting into a sense of relief.

"I'm sorry," I whispered as I stroked the buck's head and neck and the tears spilled from my eyes. In that moment, I realized that taking a life, even out of necessity, is something weighty and raw.

But this was no time for emotions because the clock was ticking. I knew other animals in the forest, including bears and wolves, could smell death from miles away and would soon come to investigate. I knelt beside the buck as I unsheathed the knife Carl had given me. I gagged a bit as I made the first incision, warmth spilling into the snow and blood steaming in the cold air. I worked quickly, my hands slick, my breath shaky. By the time I was done, my fingers were numb and my face streaked with sweat despite the cold. But I had crossed a threshold into a new world, a place where I'd live for the rest of my life: I'd ensured my own survival. I looked up at the vast Alaskan sky overhead, a sky already beginning to dim to violet twilight. I was most assuredly alone, but I was not helpless.

Fast-forward forty years and I'd spent my entire life as a hunter. And as much as I'd like to think that I've always been a damn good one, the truth is there's nothing easy or predictable about hunting. You fail as often as you succeed, and each trip is a journey into the unknown, one where the forces of nature often conspire against you. And sometimes, the obstacles that come between you and success are the ones you never saw coming.

That's exactly what happened in the summer of 2016, when I decided to head out—with the *Life Below Zero* crew in tow—on a multiday trip to hunt Dall sheep, the iconic and elusive wild sheep native to the Brooks Range and Arctic National Wildlife Refuge. Sporting a pure white coat of thick, woolly fur that allows them to melt into the snowy backdrop like ghosts, Dall sheep are exceptionally well adapted to the harsh environment of the Far North, where extreme cold, high winds, and predators shape their behavior and survival strategies. The biggest males can stand more than three feet tall and weigh as much as two hundred pounds, and their meat is prized among local hunters for both its leanness and taste. And yet, in all the years I'd lived and hunted in Alaska, I'd never taken one down.

For good reason. More than anything, Dall sheep are alpinists, high-altitude specialists that prefer the rocky, windswept ridges to the broad, flat (and much easier for humans to navigate) valleys below. For the hunter, this means an extraordinary amount of time spent in uncomfortable places marked by steep cliffs, rocky outcrops, and high plateaus, terrain that offers sheep a natural defense against wolves and grizzlies (their primary predators) and a bird's-eye view of the land around them. Sneaking up on one is next to impossible, and they escape threats by bounding up near-vertical cliffs, where other animals simply cannot follow.

Such challenges notwithstanding, I'd planned the trip for weeks. There were no guests at Kavik, the weather forecast was perfect, and I had enough money in the bank for the flights into and out of the reserve. So when the Piper Super Cub landed on the Kavik airstrip early one afternoon, I was already packed with enough gear and food to last me a week. The days to come would demand endurance and patience, and there was no guarantee of success. But the way I saw it, even an opportunity to view these majestic creatures in their native habitat was a privilege enjoyed by few. So as the plane lifted gently off the ground and we circled around to the south, my heart pounded in anticipation of what was to come.

Not long after, the pilot dropped me off on a gravel bar in an unnamed glacial river valley; the plane carrying the crew and their gear followed shortly behind. Even though it was the height of summer, the wind cut through my layered clothing, a subtle reminder that winter was never far off, a reality confirmed by the pockets of snow in shaded areas that stubbornly refused to melt.

Alaska law prohibited me from hunting on the same day I flew (scouting animals from a plane gives humans an unfair advantage), so after setting up a stationary camp in the valley bottom, I decided to head out on foot to see if I could get an idea of where the sheep might be and which direction I would head the next morning. With little else to go on other than instinct, I started walking east, making my way through the brush until I emerged onto a wide, braided streambed.

After an hour and a half of walking, the melodic song of a wolf howl echoed across the valley, as unadulterated a sound as the wild had ever produced. I stopped and listened, rooted to the spot in a combination of fear and wonder. At first, it was a lone note drifting through the summer air, but then another and another rose to meet it, a wild chorus rolling in waves across the valley.

Judging by the volume of their howls, I knew the wolves were close, but not too close. And yet as I stood there I could feel their song shifting, almost tightening around me. My heartbeat picked up, but there was no fear—not yet, anyway—just the sharp awareness that I was not alone. Lost in the moment, I tilted my head and howled back. The response was immediate—another round of calls, sharper, perhaps more defined. They heard me; they knew I was there.

I listened again, mapping their movements by sound alone. Were they hunting or just curious? It was too soon to tell. The howls shifted again, some ahead, some flanking. I tried to draw comfort from the fact that I had a Ruger on my belt but knew it would be little consolation against a pack of determined wolves. I was armed, but with the wolves drawing closer, I needed to get back to the tent. The only question was whether they would grant me passage.

I turned and walked, slowly but purposefully, in the direction I had come, scanning the landscape for the wolves, which had yet to reveal themselves to me. I crossed the streambed, crested a low hill then walked down again and into a hollow below. It was in that moment that I had a frightening realization: If the wolves did have malintent, I'd just played right into their paws.

I know how wolves hunt. The alphas of the pack send out the betas to pique curiosity and create interest in their prey. If the prey follows, they usually find they've been lured into an area—exactly like the one I was in—where there is minimal chance of escape. The wolves close in, and a few savage moments later, prey has become meal.

Meanwhile, the hollow was too quiet. The howling had stopped; the only sound was the wind filtering through the brush. Instinct prickled at the back of my neck, that primal sense that I was being watched. Hand on the holster, I turned my head slowly, scanning the trees and brush for a shadow moving between the willows.

Then, from the brush ahead, a huge shape, moving slowly but deliberately, emerged from the shadows and faced me. The alpha. He stepped into the open, his wide paws sinking silently into the earth. His coat was thick, the color of snow-dusted stone, and I could see the scars that marred his muzzle, testaments to battles fought long ago. His eyes met mine, and everything else faded away. Mercifully, I could see no malice in his gaze, just curiosity. But then the alpha made the slightest sound, and his mate emerged from the brush beside him. Then another beside her. And another. Before I knew what was happening there were a dozen wolves on the hills around me, yipping, howling, talking.

I was frozen in place, half with fear and half with wonder. Every instinct I had screamed at me to lower my eyes and make myself small, but something inside told me submission was not the answer. So I pushed through the terror and held the alpha's gaze, not as a challenge but as a message: *I am here, but I am not prey.* I knew the encounter was going to end one of two ways: Either I'd be dinner or I'd make it out alive. Only I wasn't quite ready to die. So I straightened up to make myself look as big as possible and looked directly into the big yellow eyes of the alpha. "OK," I said. "I'm going to leave now because I want to be alive tomorrow."

The alpha flicked his ears and tilted his head, and with that silent command the pack shifted. In the space of a heartbeat, they turned and melted back into the brush, vanishing like ghosts. The alpha lingered a moment longer, watching me. Then, as quietly as he came, he turned and was gone. I released a breath I didn't know I was holding and turned to walk back toward camp, my shaking hand rattling on the butt of my gun the entire time.

It was sunset when I finally made it back to camp, where I

boiled water and ate dehydrated stew and then settled in for the night in the mind-blowing wonder of the Arctic wilderness. Later that night, as the light of a billion stars shone overhead, I heard the pack, now many miles away, calling to one another again. I was alone again, but not unchanged.

The next morning I was up at 4:00 a.m. After a short breakfast, I walked for miles before I climbed a high ridge and pulled out my spotting scope, scanning the distant crags and scree fields for any indication that the sheep might be near. I spotted a small band of rams a few miles across the valley, bedded down in a rocky saddle. After noting their location and wind direction, I headed off in dogged pursuit. As I crossed the miles between us, I felt exposed, vulnerable, and clumsy, like I was the only thing moving on the ground and the rams were simply watching me slog across the marshy hummocks for pure entertainment. In the back of my mind, I knew the crew was right behind me, but as always, I tried to focus only on myself and blur them into the background.

My advance was painstakingly slow. Eventually the valley bottom gave way to rising ground, though the increase in altitude offered little respite. In fact, as the hills rose before me, the terrain became even more grueling, alternately punctuated by loose shale, steep switchbacks, and knife-edged ridges. Every step required focus; even one misplaced foot could spell disaster. I hunkered down in crevices when I could, glassing the sheep through my scope. By nightfall I was within striking distance, but the animals remained vigilant, so I eventually retreated to a concealed bivouac site and braced for a cold night ahead in my bivy sack.

When morning came, I was once again up at first light, where I inched forward, crawling over the rocks and moss separating me from the sheep. As I closed to within five hundred yards—almost close enough to get off a clean shot—my heart pounded with excitement. But just as I reached around to pull my rifle off my shoulder, the wind betrayed me and a sudden gust carried my scent up the slope. Immediately the rams snapped to attention and then bounded up the escarpment in a series of powerful, effortless leaps. Within moments, they vanished into a maze of cliffs.

I was disappointed but not crushed. The last few days had been exhausting, but a big part of the hunting experience for me had always been about the opportunity to explore another part of my Alaskan backyard. And every time I did, the journey opened my eyes to more beauty and wonder than I'd known before. Here was a world unspoiled by time, where jagged peaks rose like silent sentinels all around me. To the north and west, the tundra, now bursting in a thousand shades of green with the frenzied life of summer, rolled endlessly toward the horizon, dissected by gray-blue threads of glacial rivers that shimmered in the slanted light of the Arctic sun. Overhead, a golden eagle soared majestically on an updraft, its wings stretched wide in effortless mastery of gravity as it scanned the ground below for a quick meal.

That same wind carried the smell of eternity on its wings, a scent unlike anything I'd ever known. Pure, crisp, and untouched by human presence, it combined the peaty musk of the boggy valley bottom far below with the faint, chalky mineral scent of stone around me. Hours later, when I'd returned to my temporary camp for the night, that same breeze would carry the rich aroma of a nearby cranberry patch, and for a moment I'd be back in my little Chena cabin, that same small girl learning how to fend for herself in the great unknown.

I inhaled deeply, reveling in the simplicity of the moment and letting the solitude settle into my bones. For a precious, fleeting moment, I was nothing more than another animal in the vast, unbroken beauty of Alaska's last true wilderness. This place, I realized, does not belong to me or to any human. The Arctic is unforgiving and eternal, and yet I had become a living, breathing part of it.

I was part of it.

I let the statement echo through my brain long enough for its weight to settle. I'd lived my life largely feeling like an outsider, but in that singular moment in time and space, I was exactly where I was meant to be: not separate from the wilderness, but *within* the wilderness and *of* the wilderness. Then a movement caught my eye, a flash of white against the gray rocks far ahead. In an instant, the moment was over. The hunt was back on.

Once again adjusting my position to stay downwind, I closed in slowly, almost imperceptibly, on the sheep. Up over ridges, around rocky outcrops, and into hidden passes I tracked them. Finally, after hours of exhausting travel, I closed in on a big male grazing in an alpine basin, less than four hundred yards away. Instinctively, I dropped to my belly, inching forward until I found a stable shooting position. I steadied my breath and looked down the scope, waiting for the ram to turn sideways and offer a broadside shot.

Then, just as I was aligning the crosshairs in the scope, something happened that I would never have expected, but one that immediately reminded me that the new reality of my life was not nearly as solitary as it once was: There was a flash of red in my field of vision, followed by a voice yelling so loud that it scared away every animal for miles around.

"Wait, Sue. Stop!" it called. "*Stop!*"

Moments later, the flash of red I'd seen out of the corner of my eye was grabbing my arm, as the show's producer had decided he couldn't handle the thought of watching the sheep die.

"What in the living fu… What are you doing?" I shouted.

"I'm… I'm sorry," he stammered back. "I… I just didn't think you were actually going to shoot the sheep. We have a ton of great footage, and I thought that's where we would stop."

At first, my blood boiled. I clicked on the safety and tossed my gun down the scree slope. The past few days had been grueling, but my efforts had paid off: For the first time in my life, I was about to bag a Dall sheep. And now, in a culture clash that all too clearly defined the philosophical chasm between Alaska and LA, the moment was gone. As much as I liked the producer, he didn't fully appreciate what hunting represented to me. It wasn't TV. It wasn't sport. It wasn't cruelty. It was survival, the culmination of my knowledge, my respect for the land, and the sometimes-rugged edges of reality that defined my life.

As my blood pressure began to settle, I realized that it wasn't fair of me to expect people who'd never lived in my shoes to understand that. To the crew—as with most of the people who watched my show—food is a thing that comes from grocery stores, hidden behind plastic wrap and polite terminology. The death that inevitably accompanies that eight-ounce steak is something distant, a faraway world of blood and guts that few people entertain as they wander the meat aisle. For them, the beauty and emotion are limited to the animal itself, not in the cycle of predator and prey.

I exhaled and held the producer in my gaze. He was damn good at his job, we had developed a close friendship, and it was impossible to be mad at him. But somewhere beneath the anger, another emotion was rising up, a creeping frustration at what the moment represented. My life—at least *part* of my life—had become entertainment, and that came at the price of the kind of interference I'd just experienced. Sure, the crew was *out* of my life far more than it was *in* my life, and crew members usually did an admirable job of staying out of my business. But as I'd just been reminded, there was an umbilical cord that tethered us to one another much more tightly than I'd recognized.

I sighed and shook my head. "It's OK," I said, standing up and putting my arm around him.

And with that, I let it go. The hunt was a bust, the sheep gone, the moment lost, my gun somewhere down the scree slope. My body—still just a shadow of what it was before the bear attack—ached from days of effort. Had I thought about it longer I likely would have worried about the lack of meat in my freezers, but at the same time I knew the Porcupine and Central Arctic caribou herds would be migrating southward through the Kavik River valley in the weeks and months to come, providing me ready access to one of the world's healthiest and most plentiful meat sources.

Disappointed at the outcome of the hunt but grateful for having had the opportunity to explore another part of my big backyard, I clambered down the hill, shouldered the rifle, and started the long walk back to camp where I'd meet the bush plane the next morning. My legs were more tired than they'd been in a very long time and the bags I'd brought to transport the meat gnawingly empty, but along the way I'd gained another level of respect for the landscape and its four-legged inhabitants.

The crew never replicated the Sheep Incident, and the overwhelming majority of our subsequent interactions were positive ones, even when it came to hunting. With time we developed a wonderful working relationship. I grew accustomed to their near-constant presence in my life during the weeks-long periods when they were in camp filming, and they came to respect and appreciate me and the vagaries of my life. There would always be a cultural disconnect between us, but we had built enough bridges to keep our partnership fun and cordial, and when they accompanied me on subsequent hunts, they proved to be witnesses rather than actors in the drama.

That's exactly what happened the next summer, when a rogue grizzly bear entered camp and began to pose a serious threat to the safety of the crew and guests who were visiting at the time. The bear had been a regular presence at Kavik for months before that, and I knew by his increasingly brazen actions that things were not going to end well if I didn't put an end to his visits.

At first, the bear merely skirted the perimeter of camp; on several different occasions, I saw his massive paw prints in the mud down by the river. But as the weeks passed, the prints drew closer and closer, to the point where they were now regularly crisscrossing the narrow pathways between the buildings. In the years since I'd first come to Kavik, I'd done an admirable job of cleaning the place up, but the grizzly population of the North Slope was still *very* robust, and I had a responsibility to my guests to make sure their safety was my top priority. And with families (and children) scheduled to arrive in the next few days, bears were most definitely *not* welcome.

My choices were simple, binary: be the aggressor or the defender. My first choice had always been to defend, especially when it came to interactions with animals much higher on the food chain than myself. So if I could somehow convince the bear that Kavik was *not* a KFC and move him along on his journey, that's what I would do. Having once had my head in a grizzly's jaws, I did not want to force a confrontation I might not survive.

As part of my defensive strategy, I got on the phone that afternoon and called an old musher friend in Wiseman to see if he had any dogs he no longer needed or wanted. Bears and dogs don't get along, and I knew that if a bear wandered through camp, a giant Alaskan malamute would be my first line of defense. The next morning, Ermie—a retired sled dog who'd run the Iditarod a few times—arrived. Little did I know how quickly she'd be called into action.

A week after Ermie's arrival, the camp was bustling with people. Hunters had arrived for bear season, and I'd also invited a few local Fairbanks families up for a week, free of charge, to enjoy the glory of a North Slope summer. On top of that, the *Life Below Zero* crew was also in camp, though our several weeks of shooting had come to a close the day before and they were scheduled to head south on a charter in the morning. In the midst of all that activity wandered the bear, straight up the gravel pathway that leads from the river and directly into camp.

Ermie was out front, tethered to a line just outside the newest building addition in Kavik, a long yellow Quonset-style tent that I was now calling home instead of the ten-by-ten section of dining hall that had been my bedroom for years. I called the new building the Twinkie because it was bright yellow and full of goodness on the inside. I was sitting at my desk working when Ermie exploded into a cacophony of snarls and growls. I knew immediately what it meant.

By the time I grabbed a gun and ran outside, the grizzly—a massive male at least seven feet long from nose to tail—was knocking the poor dog around from side to side like she was a hockey puck. The sight froze me to my core. For a brief moment, I was no longer in Kavik but out on the tundra once more, the beta tossing me around like a rag doll, my hips being torn from their sockets.

Ermie's yelps snapped me out of my nightmare and set me to the task at hand: saving her life and protecting everyone else in camp, including me. After a quick check to make sure nobody was in my line of fire, I unloaded two shots at the bear's feet. I could have shot the bear then and there but may have hit poor Ermie instead. Plus, if I didn't kill the bear with my first shot, there was a very good chance he would have rampaged the camp and torn it—and everyone in his path—to shreds. A wounded bear is a dangerous thing.

Thankfully, the grizzly turned tail and sprinted out of camp, his broad, humped shoulders rolling powerfully with each stride as he crossed the river in an impossibly short amount of time, dust, moss, and gravel kicked up in his wake. Then, as quickly as he had arrived, the bear was gone, the only evidence of his visit the massive prints he left behind and poor Ermie, who was very much alive but quivering and panting with adrenaline and fear.

Once I made sure everyone else in camp was unharmed, I focused on the grim decision the encounter had engendered. I could sit back and wait, hoping the bear was scared enough by the gunshots to never return. But I'd been around bears long enough to know that their fear of humans—even ones with guns—is minimal. If that bear had his sights set on Kavik, for whatever reason, nothing was going to keep him away. I'd gotten lucky that he had first come across Ermie and not a twelve-year-old guest, but the next visit might not end the same way. After a few moments of consideration, my path forward became clear: The bear had to be eliminated.

As unequivocal as that reality may have been, it was not an easy decision. In the years after the beta attack, I'd resumed my regular hunting activities, but until that point I had staunchly avoided anything to do with bear hunting, if only to preserve my mental and emotional well-being. No matter how many years had passed, every time I thought of the attack, I relived it in chilling detail. My heart pounded uncontrollably, my hands trembled, my eyes filled with tears. I'd survived one grizzly attack; the thought of another one was too much to consider.

The dilemma weighed heavily on me. How could I kill a creature for existing in its own land, for simply following its instincts? I was an intruder here as much as he was. But as I grappled with that question, morality shifted in the face of responsibility. The guests at Kavik were, in a sense, in *my* care; their safety was my burden. The bear had made his decision. Now I had to make mine.

Serendipitously enough, bear-hunting season was set to open in three hours, and as long as I shot the bear during open season, I wouldn't have to justify my life-or-death decision to the wildlife officers in Fairbanks. I went inside the Twinkie and began to gear up for the hunt. When I'd gathered everything I needed, I sat on my bed, rifle across my lap, staring into space, alternately overcome with crushing guilt and buoyant determination. Slowly, though, determination won out and I assumed the hunter's mentality. Fear and trauma had once made me a victim; now they made me a protector.

With the *Life Below Zero* crew still in camp, I realized that the ensuing hunt might make for good footage, so I asked if they wanted to stay. Two had to go home to attend to family obligations, but the other two decided to remain and join me. One of them, a cameraman/cinematographer named John, was not only an amazing guy who'd become a close friend but an experienced outdoorsman and hunter as well. He couldn't carry a gun per network rules, but I'd feel safer just knowing he was along. The safety coordinator, Keith, who had accompanied the crew on many previous shoots, joined us as we set out on a couple of four-wheelers the moment hunting season officially opened.

For the next twelve hours, we tracked the bear across the tundra, an exhausting journey in almost every respect. We followed its tracks when we could but often lost them and were left to wander aimlessly in the hopes that we would either spot the bear from a distance or pick up his tracks once again. Physically, there were no roads to follow, just us bouncing along long-forgotten exploration roads, across shallow creek beds, and over the uneven, spongy tussocks that stretched before us forever. When we realized we were getting close to the point of no return—where we wouldn't have enough fuel for the return trip—we ditched the machines and searched on foot, picking our way carefully across the ankle-breaking humps of muskeg, through hidden pools of water, and between patches of low brush. Emotionally, although I'd come to peace with the decision to pursue the bear and had fully embraced the hunt, the memories of the beta attack haunted me, wisps of a nightmare that refused to yield no matter how hard I tried to expunge them from my memory.

After crisscrossing the tundra west of Kavik for what seemed like an eternity, eventually we crested a low hill and spotted the bear about a mile away, at the base of another low, rolling hill that disappeared to the north. The moment of truth was upon us, but before we went in for the kill, I made sure to set the ground rules with John and Keith.

"I don't expect anyone to be a hero here, boys," I said. "You know as well as I do that things can change in a hurry, and if they do, we are only responsible for ourselves, OK? Just remember that you do not have to stick around if you're uncomfortable."

After they both nodded their assent, I moved us, slowly and carefully, to a spot where we were directly downwind of the bear. Then—when we had closed to within a half mile or so—I dropped to the ground and began to belly crawl so I could get close enough for a clean shot. Luckily, the bear was fully engaged in digging up the earth, likely searching for ground squirrels or foraging for roots, and was completely unaware of our presence. I pulled out my spotting scope and focused on the bear. At 672 yards, it was still too far for a reliable shot; we needed to close the gap.

We crawled some more, our bodies rising and falling with the contours of the damp ground beneath us. The bear's back was turned to us, but every once in a while he stopped, sniffed, and looked around, only to return to his obsession. I knew that with each yard we drew closer, the danger increased, so I made sure to move as quietly and deliberately as possible. As I did, the voices of fear that had been murmuring in my head had increased to a dull roar. To quiet them, I repeated the same thing to myself over and over again. *You have to do this*, I told myself. *You have to.*

After what seemed like an eternity, I drew to within two hundred yards of the bear, more than close enough for an accurate shot of such a big target. Still, with the summer foliage in full bloom, it was difficult to get an unobstructed view of the grizzly. I wriggled into position, settled the gun's bipod (its two retractable legs) on the ground for stability, and waited. My body ached, my heart hurt, and still the bear was obstructed from my view. I could have taken a shot and hoped, but an ill-aimed bullet will do nothing more than piss off a full-grown North Slope grizzly, and I was not going to take that chance.

As we waited, I occasionally shifted position to keep my legs from going numb and my back from stiffening, which they did with annoying regularity. But when I stood up slightly to readjust my position, dark fate intervened: I coughed. I wasn't loud, and I made sure to cut it off almost as quickly as it had left my mouth, but the damage was done. The sound echoed across the landscape between the bear and me. A moment later, the grizz reared up on his hind legs, locked eyes with me, and, before I had a chance to figure out what was actually happening, dropped down and charged.

I struggled to track the bear as it ran through the brush in my direction, its broad back and golden-brown fur alternately disappearing and reappearing between the willows as it barreled toward us. In just a few seconds, it had cut the distance in half. The urge to turn and run was as powerful as any I'd ever felt, and I could feel the panic oozing from my pores as well as those of my companions. But to our eternal credit, we all stayed rooted to the spot and held our ground.

I clicked off the safety of the rifle and looked down the scope at the bear, now in a full sprint and as full of piss and vinegar as any I'd ever seen. This time there was no camp to crawl back to; it was kill or be killed.

With this hard-edged duality running through my brain—peppered with a generous helping of memory of the previous attack—I calmed myself, inhaled, and squeezed the trigger. An arc of blood sprayed several feet from the bear's body, and it collapsed. At first I thought it was a clean kill, but when the bear rose from the dead moments later, roared in rage, and began to charge once again, I believed my fate was sealed. I'd gotten lucky with the beta, but in the end, the bears would have their satisfaction. *This*, I told myself for the second time in a handful of years, *is how I die.*

Without a second to lose, I took a breath to compose myself and then looked through the scope and squeezed off another round. The bear collapsed again, and this time he didn't get up. Even so, I couldn't be sure if he was dead or alive. I watched closely for several minutes but saw no sign of movement, heard no sound of life. And yet I knew better than to approach the bear from the front: If he were still alive and I drew to within striking distance, he would have his revenge on me, no matter how extensive his injuries. More than one hunter had been killed this way, and I was not about to become a statistic, not after having apparently survived the charge, not after having survived the beta.

I knelt on the turf, shaking uncontrollably, the tears streaming down my face in torrents. The tundra was silent but for the sounds of me sobbing into my hands. Regret, pride, fear, resolution… They all rattled around inside me until I finally landed on the feeling that would carry me for the rest of the day and the days to come: acceptance. The bear was only being what it was meant to be, a wild, beautiful, dangerous force of nature.

But so was I.

CHAPTER 12

BEAUTY AND THE BEAST

John and Keith departed Kavik a few days later, and by October I was on my own again as my last guests left for the season and the echoes of human companionship faded like the summer sun. I was alone again, no longer a TV "personality" but the same raw and elemental woman who had stumbled upon this place many years before. In fact, if the passage of time had had any effect on me, it was only to deepen my appreciation for life at Kavik to levels I'd never thought possible.

At the same time, I had also come to value the *Life Below Zero* experience in ways I never anticipated. I was grateful for the time I spent with the crew, the friendships we had formed over the years, and the newfound of sense of financial security that came along with being part of the show. Such benefits aside, there was nothing I cherished more than settling into the beats and rhythm that accompanied my aloneness in that vast, wild place. Slightly unnerving at first, the silence quickly became a familiar comfort, and as the days shortened and nights lengthened, I tuned in once again to the natural rhythms of the Arctic. It was a cycle I had lived through many times, but it never got old.

Late summer and early fall was a season of preparation, and my days were measured by the practical tasks that would ready camp for the coming months of cold. I gathered and stored water; secured shelters that would lie empty and dormant until the following spring; ordered, sorted, stacked, hunted, butchered, and prepared the provisions that would keep me fed. Autumn came and went like a wisp of memory in a blaze of fiery red, burnt orange, and deep purple sunsets, and the snow that soon covered the ground would remain there for the next six months. The air grew colder with each passing day, but the land still bustled with the last vestiges of life before darkness reigned: geese lingering in tundra ponds before migrating south, loons calling sorrowfully from distant lakes, caribou herds grazing on nearby hills, and the ever-present foxes entertaining me with their playful activities at all hours of the day and night.

Then, with the inexorable descent of winter, my routine became steady, deliberate. Parts of many days were defined by survival tasks, but at the same time I was buoyed by a sense of freedom that lifted my spirits to the greatest heights imaginable. I'd left Eddie, my children, and now my grandchildren behind to make a life at Kavik, but the rewards I'd gotten in return filled my soul in ways that nothing else on Earth ever could. At night I watched the northern lights dance overhead in silent waves of green and purple, but everything else around had slowed, like the beat of a bear's heart in its winter den, to almost a complete stop.

Later that winter, I was awakened one night by a terrible ruckus coming from the wolf den on the west side of the Kavik River, a few miles from camp. At first I thought it was merely two males scrapping for hierarchy within the pack, but as the sound echoed across the otherwise silent hills I realized that one sound predominated the snarls and barks: a single wolf yowling and wailing, apparently in anguish. Eventually the pack quieted down and I was able to go back to sleep, but in the days to come the pattern repeated itself several times and always ended the same way, with the single wolf yowling, alone, in distress.

With light having returned to the Arctic sky for a few fleeting hours each day, I decided to investigate further, crossing the Kavik onto the tundra beyond, where I could get a good look at the den and pack from a safe distance. As I suspected, the male and female "alpha pair" of the pack had decided to expel another female from the pack. The ruckus I heard every night occurred when the female tried to reintegrate with the pack, something the alpha pair refused to let happen: Once the alphas expel a wolf from the pack, the decision is final, and the expelled animal becomes a lone wolf. And a lone wolf that keeps trying to reintegrate with the pack will eventually be killed trying.

Then, just as quickly as it had started, the commotion stopped, and I figured the lone wolf either was dead or had accepted its fate and moved on. The next day, though, I noticed a single set of wolf tracks in camp. The expelled wolf had apparently discovered Kavik, suspicions I confirmed when I checked the footage on a series of motion-activated game cameras I had set up around camp. But what made the wolf tracks even more mysterious were the blobs of infectious-looking goo that appeared sporadically among them. Days later, I found a bigger, bloodier pile of the gloopy material, this time with a wolf embryo inside.

That's when the metrics of the situation became clear. A wolf pack is rigid in its hierarchy and rules, and only the alpha pair—the male and female leaders of the pack—is permitted to mate to ensure that the strongest genes are passed down to the next generation. Other wolves will mate on very rare occasions, but when that happens, the pregnant females are invariably removed from the pack, often forcibly. That's what I suspected had happened to the wolf now visiting Kavik.

For the now-lone wolf, expulsion was very much a death sentence. The strength of the pack working together was the only way to take down large prey like caribou, so she was limited to scavenging and hunting small game like ground squirrels, snowshoe hares, birds, and rodents. But if I had to guess, I'd say she had little experience with hunting on her own, which meant she had very low odds of survival.

The morning after I found the embryo, I was walking back toward the outhouse when I spotted the wolf loping across the snow, just yards away from where the camp met the tundra beyond. Later that day I stumbled upon her in front of one of the bunkhouses, standing stock-still and looking directly into my eyes from twenty feet away. I cautiously slid my hand to the butt of my revolver, but the wolf remained fixed in place, just staring. I'd been around wildlife enough to know that she would just as soon eat me as befriend me, but something about the way she stared at me softened me slightly. Like me, she'd been kicked out of her family group and was now on her own, a fight for survival complicated by the fact that she was probably still pregnant and likely battling an infection, given the goo she had continued to expel around camp.

Unsure of my next move, I returned to my little office in the dining hall and called a friend of mine in Fairbanks, a wildlife biologist who was in the midst of a wolf study, one I'd helped out with the previous summer. On Scott's advice, I put some dog antibiotics on the scant remains of a frozen caribou carcass at the river's edge and then trained the game cams on the area to monitor activity around the carcass. Sure enough, when I reviewed the footage, there was Stella (the name I'd given the wolf), following our "study protocol" to a T. Two weeks later, Stella appeared healthy again, the blobs of goo no longer appearing in her tracks. But without a pack, she still had no place to go. And apparently she had accepted me as her alpha and Kavik as her den.

This was clear by the way Stella acted whenever I appeared: She made herself small in my presence, lowering her head to the ground and crawling subserviently every time she saw me. It was perhaps the most touching thing I'd ever experienced in a life full of animal encounters, but at the same time I knew that nothing good could come of Stella's perception of me as her alpha. Somehow I needed to let her know I was not her pack and that Kavik was not her place. But to do that, I had to speak her language.

A wolf's window to the world is its sense of smell, so if I was going to successfully communicate to Stella to move on, it would have to be through her nose. I began by mixing an incredibly stinky batch of random, nontoxic scents like ammonia, vinegar, and cayenne pepper, which I poured around Kavik's perimeter in an attempt to establish my boundaries. At the same time, I put on a show similar to the one I did when the beta buried the caribou carcass in camp. I chuffed. I barked. I growled. I lowered myself into a squatting position and "peed" the foul-smelling liquid onto the ground, all the while thinking how ridiculous I would look to the average person. Not long after I'd finished, Stella walked timidly over to one of the spots where I'd "peed" and did the same. Subservience, it seemed, was complete.

Though she rarely crossed the invisible boundary I'd created around Kavik after that, Stella still lingered in the terrain around camp for the remaining few weeks of winter. But as she got healthier and more independent—and as her belly continued to grow—I saw her less and less frequently. Then, when spring set in once again, the river broke up, and the days grew gloriously longer and warmer, she disappeared altogether. I was sad but encouraged. Perhaps Stella had found another pack after all.

Later that summer, I was working outside when I spotted a wolf pack crossing the hills northeast of camp. I could tell immediately from the size and composition of the pack that it wasn't the resident group that had lived in the area for years, so I had to know. I grabbed a rifle, hopped on a four-wheeler, and halved the distance between the pack and me before stopping the machine and raising my binoculars. And there, trotting along as happy as any other member of the pack, with three young pups in tow, was Stella.

I raised my mouth skyward and gave a long, loud howl. Along with the rest of the pack, Stella stopped and looked my way before turning in unison with her pups and continuing their journey across the rolling green hills. I sat there and watched them until they disappeared over the horizon and then fired up the machine and returned home. I'd never see Stella again, but my heart was full knowing she'd found a place where she was accepted.

The summer once again wound its way toward fall and the circle of Arctic life continued unabated, the same way it had for millions of years before I arrived. The crew came and went, the guests landed and took off again. Kavik was abuzz with activity, then quiet and still, my fortress of solitude in a vast and wild world that had become the cradle of my being. Dark and light, cold and warmth, struggle and relaxation, sadness and mirth, life and death. Every month, every year held each element in different measure, and I moved through them with a knowing that only comes with having lived in a place long enough to understand its very soul. Once upon a time, Kavik had been nothing more than an experiment to me, a chance to try something new when Mike Tolbert's message serendipitously found its way to me in a Coldfoot café, but in the ensuing two decades, it had become a part of my very essence. I was Kavik, and Kavik was me.

Still, there was no denying the fact that I was getting older and the physical demands of running camp weighed on me slightly more every year. I'd been charged by wolverines, mauled by a bear, and surrounded by wolves. I'd fought through blizzards, fallen off ladders, and broken more bones than I could remember. The sum total of all those experiences was a body that didn't work the same way it once had. Things ached and creaked in ways I'd never experienced before, and I knew my day of reckoning was not far off. I don't know if I ever thought Kavik would be my forever home, but with each season I realized that leaving was much closer to my future than it was to my past.

Along with my physical aches and pains came a discomfort of another kind: financial. Running any kind of operation in the far northern reaches of the planet is a monumentally expensive undertaking, but on top of that, the bulk of the camp's income was earned in the summer. That gave me three months to make most of the money I needed to keep Kavik afloat for the rest of the year, and the government always got an appreciable portion of that. Anything left over (sometimes there was and sometimes there wasn't) got set aside for the following year's operating costs.

While all of these various forces were at play in my head and heart and I danced the dance of uncertainty about my future, I was informed by the state of Alaska that my lease—which had always been "in perpetuity," meaning it was mine forever as long as I abided by its rules—was being changed to a fixed-term land-use agreement in the name of national interest. It was an important semantic distinction and one that instantly cast my future in doubt. "In perpetuity" meant forever; "fixed term" meant the bureaucrats could define the length of time I'd be allowed to operate Kavik, after which the door would be open to any interested party to potentially take my place.

When that bomb first dropped, I freaked out. Yes, my aching body had me contemplating the end of my time at Kavik anyway, but once the government backed me into a corner, I fought back like a wolverine. I was outgunned and outmanned from the start, but the odds don't matter to a wolverine. The months that followed were marked by flights to Washington, DC, meetings with congressmen and senators, and lawyers battling lawyers battling other lawyers. It was exhausting, expensive, and disheartening. And through it all, in the back of my mind I kept wondering if I was fighting for something I was ultimately going to leave behind anyway. And then another bomb dropped, one with such seismic repercussions that I knew my fate at Kavik was sealed.

Although it had still yet to be confirmed at that point, by the fall of 2024, I and the other cast members of *Life Below Zero* suspected something was up because our contracts for the upcoming season were not renewed and no crews were scheduled for filming. Then, after March 2025, when the last episode aired and we still had received no contract-renewal offers, it became obvious to all of us that the show we had filmed for over twelve years and twenty-three seasons (we filmed two seasons each year) had run its course. *Life Below Zero* was being canceled.

I'd be lying if I said I hadn't seen the writing on the wall, but the news still numbed me. In many ways I had grown to love being a TV personality, and the financial benefits of my participation, though certainly less in recent years, were still enough to keep camp afloat in an environment where costs grew more and more outrageous each year. And now it was coming to an end.

As I settled into the notion of life after *Life Below Zero,* I searched my soul for a way forward. I'd been wondering how long I could continue to serve Kavik in the way the camp deserved, and now my TV career was coming to an end too. Surely it had to be a sign.

The more I pondered my future, the clearer the writing on the wall became: It was time to go. But as obvious as those signs may have been, my heart struggled to accept the reality of my situation. A thousand questions swirled around in my head. What would life after Kavik look like? How would I make money? I still held the lease to Kavik and owned every piece of equipment on the site; could I sell those? For how much?

I checked the answers off one by one, addressed each concern, quelled every fear. I'd grown accustomed to my life on the North Slope, maybe even comfortable in some strange and exhausting way, but I had never been one to let the fear of change cripple me. So I quieted the voices of doubt in my brain and got down to setting course for the next phase of my life.

As I did, though, there was one question that refused to evaporate, for it was perhaps the most important one...yet the only one I couldn't answer: What would happen to Kavik after I left? I *knew* I would be OK; I always had been and accepted no other alternative as my fate. But what about the plants and animals of the North Slope? Who would champion their cause if Kavik suddenly became a gas and oil operation? What would happen to the land I'd called home for so long?

When I stumbled into Kavik twenty years ago, it was an unmitigated disaster. Since then I'd spent countless hours of my time and a significant portion of my income cleaning up the place. Whether it was the old equipment buried under my very feet, the vehicle parts uncovered when a flood tore the flank off a nearby hillside, or the fish dying when an unidentifiable sludge leached into the river's pristine waters from long-forgotten tanks stashed nearby, I'd done my best to address them all. But I knew there was no guarantee it would mean anything to those who followed in my footsteps. And that, more than anything, broke my heart.

I told myself that the land is bigger than any person, that Kavik existed long before I was born and would exist long after I was gone. But somehow that didn't make it any easier, didn't ease the pain of the knot in my stomach, especially when I thought about someone else sleeping in the Twinkie, playing with the foxes, splashing in the river, and making decisions about the place I'd called home for two decades.

Time, they say, heals all wounds, and the passage of the weeks and months to come softened the constant, dull ache in my heart. In time, I changed my perspective from one of regret to one of unadulterated appreciation. I came to relish every moment at Kavik in ways that were even deeper and more meaningful than I had ever known. Every bird that flew by, every patter of a fox's paw on the snow, every wisp of wind that carried the scent of the tundra across my face reminded me of the precious, delicate balance of life in that sacred place. Along the way, life became slower, more deliberate.

I'd sit up on The Perch for hours on end, simply gazing out over the land that had defined my existence for the previous two decades. Whereas I'd once filled my days with a honey-do list that would choke even the most accomplished suburban husband, now I spent increasing amounts of time just sitting and watching. And each time I did, something beautiful happened: The world began to unfold around me, a timeless work of art played out on a canvas that felt at once endless and intimate.

To the north, a small group of caribou grazed lazily on the tundra, moving ever closer to camp. Beneath me, a curious ground squirrel scurried between fuel barrels, its tiny paws kicking up dust; a gyrfalcon circled high above the ground, scanning for prey; a lone wolf moved like a shadow across the hills.

The wind rose, and what was once silence was now filled with the subtle sounds of nature in delicate balance. Beyond the borders of camp, the willows whispered in the warm breeze. Arctic terns screamed as they dove for fish in pools of the river, their wings flashing white against the sky. I inhaled slowly and deeply, soaking up every smell of that place in the hopes that I would never forget them: the damp moss and gentle wildflowers carpeting the tundra, the elemental scent of the water as it rushed over the boulders strewn across the Kavik, and—if the wind was just right—the slightest hint of salt from the Beaufort Sea and Arctic Ocean, just thirty miles away to the north.

It's a wonderful thing, you know, this Alaska of mine. It's a Beauty and it's a Beast, all rolled into one complex package. The storms and the serenity. The cold and the warmth. The life and the death. For twenty years it had all been there—in front of me, behind me, beside me. I'd only ever been the smallest part in all of it, but man, did I appreciate the part that I'd played. Low on the food chain, louder than most, aching and paining my way through my days, simply trying to survive… That's always been me. It wasn't always pretty, and lord knows I'd made more than my fair share of mistakes, but I wouldn't have had it any other way.

Kavik taught me that there's more inside me than I ever thought possible, but the Arctic taught me that nothing stays the same. The rivers carve new paths through the tundra; the caribou migrate; the seasons turn. My time at Kavik was ending, but it would always be a part of me. The skills, the lessons, the raw, unadulterated experience of living out there… I would carry those no matter where I went.

And when I do leave, I'll take one last walk along the river, past the wolf tracks and the sun-bleached remains of an old caribou kill. I'll run my hands through the soft leaves of the willows, breathe in the North Slope's air one last time. And when the moment comes, I'll leave like the wolves do: not looking back, just moving forward, slowly and deliberately, into the unknown.

EPILOGUE

There's a cabin in the woods by a river in Alaska. A girl once sought refuge there; some might even say she raised herself there. I don't know if she became a woman there, but she sure did learn a lot about herself. She learned that she could do things on her own, find her way, survive. She discovered beauty in the ordinary, ran naked in the woods, listened to the birds, stained her hands and face with berry juice, climbed the mountains. And when winter began to settle over the land like a silent sentinel, she departed that place. But it never left her heart or her mind. Not for very long, anyway.

She visited that cabin from time to time, whenever she needed to get away, whenever she needed to remind herself of who she was and of just how far she'd come. And then, many years later, when she was a grown woman who had loved and lost, traveled, birthed and raised children, somehow found success on the screens of people's TVs, and lived a large part of her life in one of the most remote places on Earth, she visited the cabin again. Only this time she found a For Sale sign nailed to a nearby tree. So without much of a thought as to what it meant beyond the fact that somewhere deep inside she knew she had to have it, she bought the cabin and the land around it. And then, when she finally realized that her life on the North Slope had come to its natural end, she returned to the cabin and made it her home.

I pulled the truck to a stop a half mile up the Chena road, got out, and then started walking toward the path I knew as intimately as if I'd walked it yesterday. There was a track cut in the woods now and I could have driven the entire way, but for this time, at least, I wanted to do it the way I had almost fifty years before, with nothing more than a backpack on my back and my feet for transportation. Minutes later, I turned the final corner on that same path through the woods, and there—my past and my future somehow wrapped together in a single, complicated knot—was my cabin. I stopped and smiled as time folded in on itself and the echo of who I once was came face-to-face with the person I had become.

The cabin was more weathered than I remembered and—like me—sagging in more places than I cared to acknowledge. The spruce logs, grayed by years of snow and wind and sun, seemed familiar yet distant, as if they'd been awaiting my return all along. The sight of it tugged something deep inside me, a combination of nostalgia, grief, and awe but, ultimately, of joy.

I pushed open the door, and the scent of wood rot and earth

rose up to meet me. I ran my fingers over the rough-hewn logs, and for a moment I was that same girl, abandoned but determined, somehow making a home in a place where the deck was stacked against her survival. And now there I was again, returning not as a desperate child but as a woman choosing her own fate. That difference settled in my chest like a warm ember. The cabin was no longer a place of survival but one of reclamation.

I walked back outside. The property had changed a lot over the fifty years that had passed since I first discovered it. My little cabin—which had once seemed so mysterious to me—had been rendered an afterthought on the property, a relic from another time that now stood in the shadow of a much newer, larger iteration of itself.

The river flowed differently now too, farther from the front door than it once did. But it still rushed and burbled with as much vigor as ever, a constant testament to the fact that while we humans come and go in this world, nature abides. It reminded me that no matter how far we travel and no matter how many places we call home, we are always in conversation with our origins. The land remembers us long after we may have forgotten it.

Perhaps, I thought, life is more like a spiral rather than a straight line, one where we are always orbiting the shadows of our past selves, coming back to them with new understanding when time and opportunity allow. The girl who lived here could never have imagined the woman who would return. And the woman who stood there now honored that girl's struggles, her pain, and her resilience…not with sadness but with gratitude and respect.

I turned away from the river, took a deep breath of the summer air, once again rich with the smell of nearby berries, and walked back toward the cabin. It wouldn't be easy, but I would do everything in my power to restore it. The cabin had once saved my life, and I planned on returning the favor. After all, that little ramshackle building was so much more than a collection of wood and nails. It was a story. My story.

Later, I sat on the front steps of the new cabin, glass of whiskey in hand, as the sun painted the sky in ever-deepening brush strokes of pink and orange. As I did, a big, black raven landed on a stump beside me, locked eyes with me, and knowingly cocked its head to one side.

"George!" I cried. Then I laughed out loud, long and hard, and went back inside to start my new life.

READING GROUP GUIDE

1. Did you move when you were a child? How do you think moving (or staying in one spot) affected your outlook as an adult?

2. Do you think you live more in the past, present, or future? Which would you prefer to live in?

3. Despite Sue's difficulties with her mother, she still loves her. Have you had any troubles with the parental figures in your life? How have you handled these situations?

4. How did you find school as a child? Was school a place where you could truly be yourself, or was it easier to show your personality at home?

5. What places in nature do you love to visit? What about those places do you love?

6. How does Sue react to her mother leaving her in Alaska? How do you think you would have reacted in her place?

7. Sue learns a great deal from Pat White and her great-grandmother. What have you learned from the mentor figures in your life? How did/do they inspire you?

8. Do you have any thoughts on the practice of trapping animals for their fur? What do you make of Sue's arguments for why she did it and why she stopped?

9. Fixing up Kavik was an incredibly daunting task in the beginning for Sue. What was her mindset during that situation? How do you go about handling difficult or complex tasks?

10. For you, does being alone equate to being lonely? When do you feel alone, and when do you feel lonely? Do you enjoy solitude, or do you prefer the company of others?

11. When Sue is experiencing the aftermath of the bear attack, she feels gratitude for her life and what she's been able to do. What are you grateful for in your life?

12. How does getting a show on National Geographic impact Sue's life and her hopes for freedom and solitude? What positive and negative experiences arise from choosing to be on the show?

13. Sue has an immense respect for nature and the natural world around her, even grieving for the bear who attacked her. Is it important to you that nature be respected and cared for? Do you believe there is enough emphasis on environmental conservation in modern society?

A CONVERSATION WITH THE AUTHOR

What was the process of writing this book like? Did you have notes to look back on or some other kind of record, or did you mainly draw from memory?

The writing of this book was monumentally difficult for me. I don't dwell on my past. I don't try to see into my own future very far, even when my past was my present. I don't drag the negativity around and keep it in my pocket. But the process of writing a book, even with a ghostwriter, is months of asking *How did you feel? What happened? How did everybody else feel?* Things that I usually don't think about. We all see things through our personal filter on life. We may all witness the same event and remember it differently. Why? Because we view life, love, hate, eagerness, romance, and regret through the filters we create over our lifetimes. I feel so much hope and love and compassion for others and myself; I even feel love and compassion for my mother, despite our difficulties. We should all try to dwell in a positive reflection of our experiences instead of hanging on to the negativity. None of us get out of this gig alive: Why turn the precious moments of life into a bath of despair? I hope people see that there's always a choice and a chance to change, to adapt, to create, and to smile. For this book, I used my memory and asked what few people are left from my past and present to add their memories. I hope I did well and that people feel the joy and laughter as well as the epic sadness that came at times.

With so many personal details and harrowing experiences, did you find it difficult to tell the stories in this book?

I don't live in the past, and there are things I don't like to talk about in detail because when I do, I am right there in the moment again. Imagine if fifty people asked you to tell the story of a bear attack, and you had to relive it like a movie each time. It's not comfortable, but I'm not the same person today as I was the day it happened, so I can do it.

Are there any projects you're working on right now or anything you're hoping to do in the future?

Yes, I am planning a journey through the Arctic that I love, to move into the twilight era of my life that I am soon to experience. I am opening a second type of camp that will be closer to my family and enable me to pass on the experiences and knowledge I have accrued so others can make use of them. I also want to see the world!

What do you feel is the most important thing you've learned from the events in your life?

That it is just that, *my life*. It is my set of memories and experiences: how I felt, feel, and will feel about it all. That there really isn't enough time to see and do it all.

What would you like readers to take away from your story?

I hope the people who need this book find it and are inspired to love themselves and be brave enough to withstand the storms in life. The storms never last forever but are powerful enough to reshape you. And to understand that you don't have to let the bad times or the hurt become your mantra. It *was*, you *are*. So go… *Be*, but be amazing.

ACKNOWLEDGMENTS

This is the moment in writing a book and publishing it where the author takes a few sentences and tries to wrap up their gratitude to those events, people, places, and things that got them to the point of writing their book.

There is a fear that you are going to miss saying something to someone, maybe several someones! My thought process is a little different, and it goes something like this…

At this point, I would like to take a moment and say thank you to *all* of the things in my life that have happened and the people, places, and roadblocks that have come up and challenged me to discover myself.

I would like to thank my mother and the people who showed me the path less traveled, the path less appreciated, and sometimes the path far too well appreciated!

We all have a Pat White, a Carl, a Mike Vlessides, and our demons, as well as our angels and saviors. We have the Lily Dolins, the Mike Cheesemans, the Benjis, the Olys, the Daniels, the Vickis, and the Joans, and these names go on and on.

If you are going to give the accolades to the positive influences, by God…in my life? I need to give them to the negatives as well. If we are judged, it is not by the things that happened to us but by the reactions we had to them.

So thank you, Gill; thank you, Romy. Thank you, Mom. Thank you, Dad, whoever you were. Thanks to the hardships, thanks to the good times, but most of all thank you, Susan, because even when you were little Susie, your reactions shaped who I have become in this moment, and I love who I am.

May you read this book with the abandon of a three-year-old with a one-hundred-dollar bill getting the snacks for a road trip on Route 66. Buckle up and hang on for the ride!

Your reaction may very well shape you, so my last thank you is to you, the reader. You are the friend and family I simply haven't met yet.

Eddie, Jennie, Jesse, all the grands, great-grands, nieces, nephews, poochies, and Georges. How *does* one count so many stars?

You don't. You gaze at them with childlike wonder and grow.

ABOUT THE AUTHORS

Sue Aikens was born in suburban Chicago, and her life took an unforeseen turn when her mother moved her to the Alaskan wilderness at the age of twelve and left her there to fend for herself. From there she embarked on one of the most memorable modern-day tales of resilience and determination ever told, surviving on the trademark tenacity and grit she displayed even as a young girl. Wife, mother, entrepreneur, trapper, hunter, Arctic adventurer, and unlikely star of *Life Below Zero*, Sue lives in both Kavik, Alaska, and near the Chena River by Fairbanks, directly beside the once-derelict trapper's cabin she made her home during the first few months of her survival tale. *North of Ordinary* is her first book.

Alexis McKeown

Michael Vlessides is the bestselling author and coauthor of thirteen books, including *Surf When You Can*, *Survive!*, *The Ice Pilots*, and *Will to Live*. He spent years traveling the Arctic from Baffin Island to Kavik but has no problem with the beaches of Hawaii, either…as long as his wife, Caroline, is right there beside him.